# Praise for *What We Can't Burn*

"It's rare to see a book that actually tackles competing conceptions of political economy in good faith—and does so not only with intellectual sophistication, but with interpersonal complexity . . . This book will prove a useful gem to those working through what they believe—and what they might have to learn to believe—for making another world possible for us all."

— TAWANDA MULALU, author of *Please make me pretty, I don't want to die: Poems*

"A courageous travelogue offering tales from the journey to climate justice. The core wisdom at the heart of their shared narrative, is that the road to economic transformation passes through self-awareness, humility, deep listening, and a commitment to building a better world together. Their very friendship is their core contribution to the climate movement, showing that by healing the wound of a climate crisis we can build something enduring, something we can't burn."

— BRACKEN HENDRICKS, co-founder of Working Power & Evergreen Action, and partner J.M. Forbes & Co.

"An urgent guide in an era of rampant discord, this book serves as a blueprint for building coalitions dedicated to a healthier society, whether in climate justice or other vital movements."

— SOL STREET, global social impact strategist and co-founder of The Meteor

"For many involved in the climate movement, a certain paralysis takes hold when we fully commit to understanding the enormity of the situation our species finds ourselves in. *What We Can't Burn* confronts this paralysis head on, speaking across audiences and generations to offer a beautiful story of friendship and the understanding that comes from respect and care."

— AJA TWO CROWS, project manager, Center for Earth Ethics

"A richly textured and deeply personal account of intertwined lives, this book shows us environmentalism's roots in local histories, habits, and aspirations."

— AJANTHA SUBRAMANIAN, Professor of Anthropology, The Graduate Center, City University of New York

"This is required reading for students, educators, university presidents, and concerned citizens alike."

"This is a truly unique story—about two young people who couldn't be more different in their backgrounds and outlook on life—who took the time and courage to really listen to each other. In doing so, they discovered that magical space, beyond judgment, where humanity exists and change truly happens. Read this book if you desire to change the world."

"A dialog between two brilliantly smart young friends . . . It's a rare pleasure to witness two such capable spokespeople, who represent totally different perspectives, grapple with ideas, values and contradictions and emerge with deeper understanding."

"In the fight for our climate and energy future, everyone's favorite solution, whether technological or political, top-down or bottom-up, seems like a dangerous oversimplification to someone else. Yet the scale of the challenge means that giving up on big-tent cooperation is riskier still. Linked by conversations, divided by mutual frustrations, bound by moments of joy, Driver and Osborn show us that this paradox is the point—and that the only way to stop talking past one another is to keep on talking."

"In a time of such urgent climate crisis—an undeniably intersectional issue that brings key components of society and capitalism into question—this is a necessary read . . . This book helps bring some much-needed hope about how we can all find common ground."

"A compelling joint memoir . . . Both conversational and informative, their recollections reveal how even the staunchest of opinions can be changed and a consensus achieved through discussion, empathy, and information sharing, thereby achieving goals that are vital for humanity."

# What We Can't Burn

# What We Can't Burn

*Friendship and Friction in the*

*Fight for Our Energy Future*

Eve Driver & Tom Osborn

 WESTWOOD
PRESS

Printed in Canada on 100% recycled, FSC-certified paper

Library of Congress Control Number: 2024934533

Driver, Eve, author. | Osborn, Tom, 1995-, author.

What we can't burn: friendship and friction in the fight for our energy future /
Eve Driver and Tom Osborn.

Portland, OR: Westwood Press, 2024.
Identifiers: ISBN: 978-1-958510-03-2 (hardcover) | 978-1-958510-05-6 (ebook)
Subjects: LCSH Driver, Eve. | Osborn, Tom, 1995-. | Global warming--Prevention. | Climatic changes. |
Clean energy. | Energy transition. | BISAC BIOGRAPHY & AUTOBIOGRAPHY / Memoirs |
BIOGRAPHY & AUTOBIOGRAPHY / Environmentalists & Naturalists | BIOGRAPHY &
AUTOBIOGRAPHY / Social Activists
Classification: LCC GE55 .E57 D75 2024 | DDC 363.7/0092--dc23

10 9 8 7 6 5 4 3 2 1

Interior design by Morgane Leoni

www.westwoodpress.com

For my family and friends,
my teachers,
the tree I used to climb, and those who know the world is broken
and still find so many reasons to dance.




To Eve.
To Mama.
To Baba.


*Decolonize the mind.*

# Contents

# Preface

———

# Tom

## Nairobi, Kenya
### FEBRUARY 2015

Amok was late. I had been sitting at the Java House coffee shop next to the flea market we call Toi for nearly two hours. But that wasn't surprising. After all, don't we say *haraka haraka haina baraka*? There is no hurry in Africa. When Amok finally arrived, he was panting, but not in the way one might after attempting to arrive on time for a meeting with their boss. And he was unkempt, which was rather odd. Even though Amok lived in what many considered the poorest slum in the world, one could always count on him to wear a bright red tie over a well-ironed, buttoned-up shirt neatly tucked into black trousers. But today, his tie hung loose around his neck, and a tiny bit of shirt stuck out of his pants, untucked. Amok seemed panicked.

He sat down just as the waiter brought me my bill. I, too, was running late for my next meeting. He insisted I cancel it. Gathering himself, he ordered an orange juice and his usual heated-up lemon poppy muffin. But the warmth and baritone radiance that usually marked his presence were absent. He was nervous; I could feel it. I could feel it in the way my gaze—for the first time—subdued his. I could feel it in his legs, restless beneath the table. This was a different Amok. I wanted to ask him what was the matter, but I did not. I could not. Even if he was my employee, he was fifty, and I had only just turned twenty. In Kenya, we are taught to respect our elders.

Amok eventually found his voice that afternoon in February 2015. And when he did, he spoke four words that have haunted me ever since: "We cannot do it." These four words lingered in my memory four years later when I traded the Java House—nestled next to the open-air market on a by-street of Ngong Road in Nairobi—for a Starbucks at the bustling intersection of Massachusetts Avenue in Cambridge, famously known as Harvard Square. And they still echoed fresh in my mind—like a movie clip—eight years later when I returned to that same Java House. Why do cognitive scientists insist our brains do not function like video cameras?

On that humid Wednesday, I had wanted to ask Amok what he meant. (Surely, this was the time to employ the authoritative voice I had been cultivating.) But I did not. Instead, after swiftly finishing his muffin and orange juice, Amok informed me there was someone I had to meet and insisted I come with him. Suddenly, the tables had turned. Now it was I who felt panic rising, whose previously steadfast gaze was jittery with unease. His request sounded more like an order, his words dominating the space between us, subduing me. All I could do was follow.

Amok is a short man with a heavy, rotund build and a bald head that often reflects the equatorial sun—thanks to a very generous amount of Vaseline. How odd a pairing we must have made that day as we walked hand-in-hand past the Shell Petrol station that marks the beginning of Toi: a short, round man and a tall, lanky boy whose long hair was beginning to twist into dreadlocks. We were walking to Kibera.

I've always found a certain pleasure in walking to Kibera, a thirty-minute walk from my office on the "better side" of Ngong Road. The walks fill me with an indescribable energy. Sometimes, it feels like a surge of giddy anticipation, while other times, it settles me into a steady, comforting rhythm. But each time, it offers a pulse of life that makes me feel truly alive. A University of Chicago economist once wrote that if people could choose where they were born, no one would choose a place like Kibera.

And why should they? Why would anyone choose to live in a place the size of New York's Central Park, with three hundred thousand people packed like sardines? Who would choose to live on two dollars a day, bound by the brutal confines of the monster that is extreme poverty? Who would choose to live in a place where the daily menu features unemployment, HIV and AIDS, crime, sexual violence, a lack of running water, and inadequate medical care? I could see why the economist wouldn't want to trade his place in the ivory tower for what seems like a pallid gutter. But his analytical assessment ignores the human experience in favor of numbers and statistics. There is an excitement in the faces of the children running around, inventing all manner of games, making merry with whatever they can find. There's an energy, a palpable innovation within the resilience of the young men and women who constantly make life work against the odds. There's a hope in Kibera, a belief that tomorrow will be better than today. And perhaps it is this hope that has always attracted a dreamer like me to a place like this.

That afternoon, Amok and I took a left at the Law Court building toward the small, iron-sheet structure that served as Amok's office. The sun's intensity left beads of sweat on my forehead, the heat making each step heavier than the last. I could smell the distinct, acrid air of Kibera: the sting of feces and urine blended with the sour smell of rainwater-soaked earth, the dense decay of rotting food, and the sundry waste that had found its final resting place here. This was the signature scent of Kibera, unsettling yet familiar.

Inside Amok's makeshift office, a solitary light bulb hung precariously from the ceiling, its weak glow only illuminating half the room. Through the feeble light, I could make out a table pressed against the wall, strewn with the remnants of past endeavors. As my eyes adjusted to the dimness, the outlines of two figures materialized from the shadows. Their presence hung in the air like an unspoken question, leaving the atmosphere thick with a tension Amok did little to dissipate.

With a gesture made more out of compulsion than hospitality, Amok pulled four chairs around the wooden table. His voice carried an undertone of unease as he introduced me. I was the boss, he said. His words echoed around the room, magnifying in the silence. The figures turned towards me, their eyes flashing with anticipation.

Maybe the cognitive scientists are right after all, and our brains don't work like video cameras. I don't remember much after we settled around that wooden table. What I do remember is the weight of the silence, an ominous shroud that seemed to drown out all other senses. I remember the pounding of my heart, as relentless as the beat of West African *tum-tum* drums, and Amok's voice, brittle with anxiety as he introduced the shadows: the charcoal cartel.

We had made the wrong enemies, one of them said. His words hovered in the semi-darkness—a cloud of impending doom. What do you do when you make the wrong enemies?

If we knew what was good for us, they continued, we would leave Kibera. There was no detailed explanation, no elaborate justification. Even now, eight years later, I do not know if it had been a request, a threat, or a warning. Maybe it was some combination of the three. Maybe the truth lay in what was left unsaid. But the little that was said shattered the careful balance of the room. The truth, the reality of our predicament, had been laid bare: two years, countless dreams, a $200,000 investment—all gone. Demolished in minutes.

How many walks had I taken through Toi into Kibera? How many women had I met selling charcoal packed in small yellow tins under the shade of a Safaricom umbrella? I never anticipated that as I walked each night, countless trucks—packed to the brim with charcoal-filled gunny (burlap) sacks—were beginning their own journeys to Kibera. Some came from smallholder Maasai farms, others from the dry countryside of the Swahili coast or the small fields surrounding the sugarcane plantations in Western Kenya. Still others—the ones that mattered—began their journeys from the Badhaadhe District in Somalia.

It is in Badhaadhe that al-Shabaab, a jihadist terrorist group in East Africa with strong links to al-Qaeda, turns life-giving trees into life-threatening fuel. The process begins with the acacia tree, an icon of the African landscape. With their twisted trunks armored with thorns and crowned with a lush, flat canopy, acacias can endure the harsh, arid conditions of the Somali plains. Yet it's precisely this resilience that marks them for demise: their dense, hard wood is perfect for charcoal production. Armed with axes and machetes, young men strike at the acacia, their blows creating a discordant symphony of metal meeting wood. Bit by bit, the tree is stripped of its branches and reduced to a shadow of its former self until its lone trunk is brought down with the same brutal efficiency. Once the acacia succumbs, its branches and trunk are chopped into smaller, manageable pieces that are then piled into a large, shallow pit—a makeshift kiln. The pile is set alight, the flames licking hungrily at the wood. But before the fire can fully consume its meal, the pit is smothered with soil, cutting off the oxygen supply and arresting the process midway. The pit is left undisturbed for several days, allowing the residual heat to complete the transformation. What remains is a mountain of blackened wood, a testament to a life once lived. This half-burnt wood is charcoal.

The reason for al-Shabaab's interest in the charcoal trade is as clear as the noonday sun over the Somali plains: charcoal is not a luxury; it's a necessity, a staple fuel for countless households across East Africa, not unlike the one in which I grew up. This consistent demand provides al-Shabaab with a ready market—an endless cycle of unwitting consumers lining up to indirectly fund the very terror they wish to evade. What's more, the opportunity for export extends outside of East Africa, across the Indian Ocean, and into the Gulf nations. Al-Shabaab turns the acacia tree, once a symbol of life and endurance, into sacks of black gold. In 2014, the United Nations Environment Programme estimated that al-Shabaab was reaping between $38 million and $56 million per year from this charcoal trade. Amidst decades of conflict and turmoil in Somalia, the industry thrived in the shadows, unregulated and unchecked. Al-Shabaab exploited the rampant corruption in neighboring countries, collaborating with local cartels to export charcoal across Kenya, South Sudan, and Uganda and further to the markets of the Gulf.

These two men were part of this well-oiled machine. Part of me wanted to explain that GreenChar—the clean cooking company I had founded with my friend Ian after high school—was too small a player to matter to them. That in a country where 80 percent of households used charcoal, there was enough space for us to co-exist. I desperately wanted to impress upon them the seriousness of my venture in Kibera, to show them the market analysis and the impeccably assembled twelve-slide deck that had captivated my American investors. I wanted to share the damning statistics from the World Health Organization that illustrated the slow, silent death of nearly four and a half million women in places like Kibera; their lives snuffed out prematurely due to dirty wood fuels. Perhaps if I had shared the story of my mother—how the smoke from the charcoal had infiltrated her bronchioles, transforming the mundane act of breathing into a life-threatening battle that left her with ongoing respiratory tract infections—it might have swayed them. Would slide #6—with its grotesque depiction of our dying Earth, bleeding from the relentless assault of pollution—have changed their minds?

I don't know. Maybe.

Amid the tension, Amok's employee, Atieno, walked in with refreshments. It is a Kenyan custom for visitors to drink tea, and Atieno remembered that I took my Kenyan chai without sugar. In the silence that followed, the four of us sipped tea and nibbled at *mandazi*. Amok—appearing to have somewhat recovered—attempted to lift the mood with jokes, including one of a white American woman who, too timid to inform her Kenyan hosts of her lactose intolerance, turned a vivid shade of red after consuming two cups of the traditionally milky chai. Once we had drained our cups and the mandazi were nothing more than crumbs, we shook hands, and the two men departed.

The only thing that was clear to me on that Wednesday afternoon, and remains clear to me today, was that the energy and spirit that led me to found GreenChar had evaporated, leaving a void I've struggled to fill ever since. *Nchi ina wenyewe.* Our country has its owners—I was not one of them.

There's an indefinable sensation tied to loss and heartbreak, to watching something you've nurtured and committed your life to crumble. It's as if you are standing on the edge of a cliff, peering into the depths that have consumed something you hold dear. The world seems to slow down. Every laugh, every victory, every triumph crawls across your mind's theater like a tragic drama. Yet, the height of the torment is not when the loss actually occurs or when the heartbreak fully settles in. It's at the moment you realize, with a gut-wrenching certainty, that the loss is unavoidable. For me and GreenChar, that moment had arrived.

# Eve

## Cambridge, United States
### AUGUST 2016

I pulled onto campus in a school bus full of filthy 18-year-olds. When the brakes announced we'd arrived, I opened my eyes to find I'd fallen fast asleep on the shoulder of a friend I'd met six days earlier. I sat up quickly, wiping my face to check for drool. For a second, groggy, I couldn't remember whether I was supposed to feel embarrassed now. But my friend laughed, and then I did too. As everyone stood up around us, we shared a look that seemed to marvel at how recently we'd all met, and at the glorious possibility of sudden intimacy between strangers. As we all filed onto the quad lawn—rimmed by the tall brick dorms we hoped would soon feel like home—the possibilities made me feel fearless.

None of us had showered in a week—I think that was part of it. We'd just hiked deep into the New Hampshire woods on one of Harvard's 'pre-orientation' programs that takes freshmen camping the week before school starts. When it was time to go our separate ways and find our dorm rooms, we all exchanged long hugs that reeked of body and dirt, and I swear it was our smells that made those hugs last longer: nothing to prove, everyone at the mercy of their glands. The short, neat grass of the lawn seemed to cry out as we walked across it like it envied our brief chance to be wild.

The woods have always done it for me. It's the trees themselves, but also what they do to us when we're among them, the way they force us to really see ourselves and one another. Growing up outside Boston, my summers were for trail runs and campfires and acoustic guitars. They were for reading nature poems in my carrot garden—sticking my fingers into the soil and trying to feel the pulse of all the life I'd been told was down there. There was something to this that, for better or worse, bordered on religion: a clarity, or maybe a purity, that in the thick of human worlds was lost. And we had gotten so gorgeously high that final night before college off nothing but the naked realness of it all, off being stuck out there with strangers and no screens. So many tears of laughter had choked me that week as I prepared to settle into college, in the mood to fall in love with it.

And I did. At their best, liberal arts colleges are like Disneyworlds for brains: if you want, you can let yours drag you around by the hand like an eight-year-old just tall enough to ride Space Mountain. I thought I'd study international relations, but the course catalog lured me to a major that let me study the world's cultures of environmentalism through the lenses of the social sciences and humanities. I took classes about the History of Science—which nuked the high school curriculum categories—and the ways we've come to think about nature and our planet.

However, I wasn't prepared for my courses to have me thinking less about carrot gardens and more about fossil fuel companies. "Climate change"—oof—had always seemed horrifying but lifeless. I'd thought it was mostly about reducing food waste and recycling, and I cared about it only in the sense that I wished it wasn't happening.

But the more I learned, the more I understood that it is also about power. I read books about how scientists discovered the link between oil and climate change in the 1970s and tried to sound the alarm, and how oil companies worked hard to ensure no one believed them. I read about the way colonialism destroyed so many cultures' ways of living in balance with the ecosystems around them and how capitalism has deemed both trees and people worthless unless they are "productive." At every turn, it seemed, the history of nature was intertwined with the history of exploitation—both of Earth itself and of the people who loved it most.

As I watched all sorts of "-isms" congeal into a single, dark, and intractable mass, hovering over a world I'd once felt thrilled to inhabit, it became clear that the real problem with climate change was that it was making all our other problems worse. The result? A lucky few would be left to recline on chaise lounges around Lake Michigan while droughts, storms, and rising seas tore vulnerable communities apart. And the fact that political and business leaders in my own country were not just allowing but facilitating this process was devastating.

I believe "What the fuck?" was my initial reaction, but I didn't know where to go from there. My classmates and I submitted term paper after term paper into a void with no echo. In most classes, "What can we do?" was not a question we were pushed to ask or answer. And the responsibilities of the university seemed to end at the classroom door. As soon as we walked out onto the well-manicured lawns, the new, dystopian light our learnings had cast upon them was ours to either sit with or shake. The options for taking action seemed to fan out vaguely in the distance, all of them feeble in the face of corporate apathy.

But in my junior year, I made a friend who pushed me to pick one. From the moment we met, Tom drove me crazy—delighting in all the ways he found to unsettle me, then drawing me closer, flooring me with these raw flashes of truth that both freed and unwound me. He convinced me that reading books—which had become what I did all day, peeling oranges in a dim library room as I wilted under the weight of the Anthropocene—wasn't enough. And as we began to orbit faster and faster around one another, wrestling with our distinct understandings of the energy system and what it would take to transform it, I felt a peculiar force begin to thrum between us and within myself.

When I learned about the fossil fuel divestment campaign on campus, I joined it. What I didn't expect was that it would almost cost me the same friendship that had inspired me to do something in the first place.

# Introduction

———

# Tom & Eve

How pathetic and worthwhile it is to be a young person with strong convictions about the planet and what's destroying it. Tom grew up certain that if any white person were going to stop climate change, it would be Elon Musk, not Greta Thunberg, while Eve believed the lack of climate action was about politics and special interests and that the answer was truth-telling and people power.

When we first met in college, we did not get along. Despite our shared interest in what has come to be called the "just energy transition," the contrast between our viewpoints felt radical. Between our distinct lexicons of entrepreneurship and activism, drastically different cultures, unique relationships to the word "capitalism," and the ways class, race, and gender shaped our identities, we found ourselves looking at the same problem through separate lenses—ones that left us feeling like nemeses. It was weird. We felt dumb once we got over it. And eventually, we came to see how much the other could teach us.

But just as we did, we began to notice that all around us, others were fighting similar fights based on similar misunderstandings. For so long, the climate change "debate" had been a backward battle over whether it was even happening and if fossil fuels were responsible. But as we graduated into the chaos of 2020, there were finally a myriad of real debates centered around what we should actually do about it: Shareholder activism? Carbon taxes? Infrastructure bills? Venture capital for new technology? Nuclear? It became clear that far beyond just the two of us, the chorus of voices calling for "climate action" had serious rifts when it came to deciding what that "action" ought to look like.

We started writing this book, in part, for ourselves—because even after the dust had settled around our own little drama, we'd both been changed in ways we still didn't understand. But we saw it all the way through because we felt for all those coming of age around the world. Those asking, "Who am I?" "How does change happen?" "What role can I play?" without the benefit of a friend to open their mind and make them laugh when it all gets too heavy. This book is for all those trying to figure out how the world works while at the same time learning how it's broken. It's for those grappling with how to close the staggering gap between how it *does* work and how it *should*. This struggle can be painful and alienating—for children and parents, students and teachers, colleagues and friends. We wanted to share our experiences and offer others the book we wish we could have read.

We hope it arms readers with useful tools and ideas to make change despite the odds stacked against them—and provides insight into what activists and entrepreneurs can contribute to this wild moment in which we find ourselves. We also hope it adds some texture to the concept of environmental justice and illustrates the bumbling but powerful ways we can carry revolutionary ideas out of scholarly circles and into the world beyond. We wrote it in alternating chapters because it's about conversation; the climate crisis demands radical and uncomfortable forms of cooperation between people with all kinds of reasons not to trust or talk to each other. We hope it sheds light on what works and what doesn't and decenters the usual voices that often dominate these debates.

But in the end, this is a story. It's about making and keeping a friend as the world shifts under our feet. We tell this story in detail because we think the details matter; skip to the Epilogue if you're more interested in the conclusions we arrive at than the roads we took to get there. We hope you don't, though, because you might miss the point—which is more about being human amid the heat of a burning world. As two people from opposite sides of the planet, brought together through pain, both shared and distinct, we believe there can be beauty in that, even as there's horror.

# Part One

———

---

# Eve

## Cambridge, United States
### DECEMBER 2018

It was midnight on a Wednesday, and time to go home. I plunged my fists through the sleeves of my parka, heaved on my backpack, and told Oliver, "Well, I'll keep you posted."

I closed his door softly behind me and began making my way through the suite's common room. I'd been friends with Oliver since freshman year and watched him and his roommates accumulate all the doodads that now adorned their junior year space: in one corner, the banjo from Ian's stint in the mariachi band; in another, the mannequin Sean had bought for a prank war. They seemed to like living among an array of conversation starters—in a shrine to the eclectic and unusual.

I'd just about reached the suite's main door when it opened in my face. I froze. A tall and narrow man filled the door's frame, his hair falling around his face in chaotic dreadlocks and his long arms extending a bit too far beyond his sleeves. A tiny, empty-looking backpack dangled off his shoulder, but the way he carried himself seemed more befitting of a briefcase. He looked too old, or too *something*, to be a college student.

"Tom!" I said, startled. "How's it going?" I knew his name, but he was the one roommate here who I hadn't yet met.

He stood there with a straight face. After a moment, he said coolly, "Eve Driver."

This sounded more like a threat than a greeting, and I suddenly felt compelled to explain myself—that I'd been here to meet the new fish Swimothy before winter break, and I was just on my way out. I said this all too quickly, and Tom's raised eyebrows seemed to suggest he was pleased with himself for having this effect on me. He just stood there, saying nothing.

After a moment, I stiffened. He was still staring me down, so I met his gaze, beginning to feel annoyed at this steely little bit of his, annoyed at myself for falling for it. Just then, Oliver's bedroom door cracked open.

"Do you two know each other?" he asked, entering the common room. He smirked as he sat down on the arm of the couch, as though he felt this would be a funny interaction to watch unfold.

"Kind of," I said, still looking at Tom as I said it, hoping it sounded like a bold assertion of ambivalence.

Tom remained expressionless in the doorway.

"Tom, Eve's going to Kenya over winter break," Oliver said after a moment.

This, it seemed, clarified nothing. It was true; I'd just been telling Oliver that I was hoping to go to Kenya in a couple of weeks. My friend had asked me to be her research assistant there. Her grant would cover my flights, but I wasn't sure my budget had room for the hotel where she and the other researchers would be staying. Oliver had advised me to "get creative"—the advice he seemed to offer in every situation.

"Tom is from Kenya," Oliver added. "He'll be there over winter break too."

At this point, Tom let the door close behind him. With a single motion, he let his coat and backpack fall onto an armchair, leaving the sleeves still in the straps.

"And why is it that you will be gracing my country with your presence?" he said, as he went to sit on the couch beside Oliver. First, his dorm room, and now his country. What other spaces of his did I plan to invade without consulting him? Oliver laughed, but once again, I felt the need to explain myself.

I'd be working with a gender violence prevention program, I told him, in Kisumu. I'd be helping to implement it and collecting data on its effects.

Tom seemed to sense my relief at having an answer to his question and bristled at it. In hindsight, I'm sure he would have said, "What would we do without you noble Americans?" had he not bit his tongue.

I was alone now by the door, overheating in my parka, trying to figure out a polite way to leave.

But when Tom spoke again, his voice had softened.

"Where will you be staying?" he asked.

I laughed a bit, glancing at Oliver. "That's the part I'm still figuring out."

For the first time that night, Tom didn't skip a beat.

"You can stay with my family," he said. "And you can visit my village. My tribe will sacrifice for you a goat."

My eyebrows went up. I glanced over at Oliver to see if this, too, was a joke. Then I looked back at Tom. Both of their faces were earnest.

"Tom. Wow. That's really generous."

Now his eyes looked weary, benevolent—like they were replaying some series of events in his inner world that I couldn't even begin to guess at. "Thank you," I added.

That night, I walked home on the snow-crunchy median; I could only spot the black ice when it was directly under the streetlamps. I didn't know if I trusted Tom, but I wanted to. I loved the idea of learning about Kenya through the eyes of his family; in the past few years, I'd done four or five homestays across Africa, Europe, South America, and Asia, and still kept in touch with some of the families I'd stayed with. As I shuffled home in the cold dark, my ears gently numbing, I couldn't help but feel the familiar glow of the prospect of adventure.

I booked my flight a day later. All I had to do now was figure out whether before or after the goat sacrifice would be the better time to mention I was a vegetarian.

# Tom

## Nairobi, Kenya
### DECEMBER

I was born on a sugarcane farm in the heart of a rural Kenyan village called Nyabera on an early Sunday morning in June. Ordinarily, they would have named me Omondi, "he who was born in the morning," but instead, they gave me two white names: Tom Osborn. Baba says it's because they'd met an American missionary in Migori a few weeks before I was born.

Eve was going to be in Kisumu, and so I suggested she might want to visit Nyabera—only three hours away—while she was there. I invited Eve partly because Oliver thought it'd be cool for her to visit and partly because, to be honest, I was curious about her. I didn't know if Eve would like Kenya. Would she like our *nyama choma*, the roasted goat meat that is the staple of Kenyan weekend life? What about *ugali*, plain maize flour boiled down until only a semi-hard ball is left? At the time, I had many white friends at Harvard, but none had visited Kenya. I didn't have a benchmark.

There are no white people in Nyabera. The first time I brought a white person to Nyabera, there had been a party. The village dancers dressed in their colorful costumes and danced to the tunes and melodies of the *orutu* and the rhythmic pounding of drums. Women let out ululating cries, their shoulders and hips swaying with an intensity usually reserved for important rites like dowry negotiations. The men had kept their composure, cloaking their excitement behind austere expressions, as is expected of them in our culture.

Why do white people come to Africa? This question first crossed my mind during primary school, where our textbooks recounted tales of post-colonial white adventurers in the vast African terrain. To us, these stories were less thrilling adventures and more comedic missteps. Like the story of the well-intentioned German in Tanzania who, astounded by a community that lived alongside a fertile riverbank but did not cultivate crops there, saw an opportunity to intervene. It is said that the German started his own farming venture only to watch in disbelief as a marauding herd of buffalo laid waste to his carefully tended harvest. But one had to give him credit—at least he was trying to improve things for that Tanzanian community.

The first white person I ever met was Jacob, a tall Danish man in his mid-twenties with the blond hair and blue eyes of the white people in American movies. I met him during my final year of secondary school at an event called Innovate Kenya, where my friend Ian and I were showcasing our clean cooking fuel project. Jacob and his colleagues had founded Innovate Kenya, and their mission was to "unleash the innovative spirit of Kenyan youth." They were here to help us solve our problems like good white people should. That is what the textbooks told us, anyway. That is what Baba told me as he made me type grant proposals for his many business ideas on our cathode-ray tube monitor at home. Each addressed to white people in Europe and America whom Baba had never met but who he was convinced existed and had the financial means to eliminate our challenges. That is also why Ian and I immediately approached Jacob with our clean cooking fuel idea. He was as white as it got, and fortune doesn't strike twice.

Can one truly grasp the depth of pain in the absence of lived experience? I could tell Jacob about the history of charcoal use in Kenya. How firewood, once our go-to source of fuel for generations, had, with the rigors of the modern world, been replaced with the cheaper yet environmentally damaging charcoal. How it had become the primary source of cooking fuel for roughly 80 percent of Kenyan households—from the sun-bathed villages of the Rift Valley to the coastal settlements by the Indian Ocean. Or I could paint him a picture of the tins and sacks of charcoal that sat beside black hills of dust along the road in Awendo, where my family and I lived from the time I was five until I was fourteen.

On most days, I would make the five-minute walk to Min Otieno's mound of charcoal along the only tarmac road that passed through town. But sometimes, Min Otieno's stock ran dry. On those days, I would have to walk on to Makaa Ndogo, a charcoal market where women, swathed in frayed, charcoal-hued garments bore the unmistakable marks of their trade—their complexions darkened by the sun and their hands stained with soot. Black, it seemed, was the dress code for Makaa Ndogo, and even the trench separating the reddish-brown murram road from the charcoal-laden hills complied with this monochromatic aesthetic.

During those trips to Makaa Ndogo, I often prayed I would meet the man they called "Osama." Legend had it that every morning, Osama would strap three enormous sacks of charcoal into his bicycle's rear rack and pedal some sixty kilometers from Oyani to Awendo. It was said that if Osama didn't make his trip, the hearths of Awendo would grow cold. And sometimes, I found myself wishing that Osama had not made his trip that day. That I'd find the stalls empty. That I'd return home unburdened by the weight of a two-kilo charcoal bundle wrapped in black polyethylene. That I'd not have to transfer four to ten lumps of charcoal to our *jiko*, that trusty black ceramic cookstove. That I'd not need to scour our home for old newspapers, twigs, or discarded scraps of paper to stuff into the stove's base for kindling. That I'd not need to strike a match and fan the nascent flames with a plastic plate until billows of dense, white smoke seized my lungs and stole my breath in a fit of relentless coughing—one minute, two minutes, ten minutes—until the charcoal's stubborn black finally surrendered to a yellow-orange. But Osama always made the trip, without fail, every single day.

Nature, like humanity, is filled with deep contradictions. Charcoal breathes warmth into our homes and fuels our jikos, but it also fills our lungs with smoke as it chokes the life out of the planet. It is the end and beginning of a devastating cycle whereby environmental degradation leads to decimated livelihoods, which leads to more unabated deforestation—each step simultaneously magnifying and magnified by the ravages of climate change. This is what I told Jacob. I told him that 80 percent of Africa's energy needs were met through biomass fueled by deforestation. That every year, nearly 130,000 acres of trees are cut down. I told him that in Africa and Asia, the burning of solid fuels like charcoal contributed to 60–80 percent of black carbon emissions.

But what about the people? What about the human toll? What about the 4.3 million lives lost annually—primarily women and children—from inhaling toxic fumes, the result of burning dirty fuels? Did it matter that those emissions ranked as the world's fourth highest health risk? All of this I kept to myself. I didn't tell Jacob how my mom lost a piece of herself every time she stooped over her jiko, her lungs eroded by particulates from the charcoal that inflamed her respiratory system.

My dad was right: white people can move mountains. Jacob, through Innovate Kenya, gave Ian and me a $5,000 grant to launch GreenChar upon our high school graduation in December 2013. Jacob also flew me to New York City, where I met more white people who moved more mountains. With the additional funds, we built a factory and hired twenty people, including Amok. We helped thousands of families acquire clean cooking fuel and cookstoves to save their lungs and the planet.

———

Eve was a different white person, and she was visiting as a guest. I did not expect her to move mountains. In fact, I was very suspicious of the work she and her colleagues were doing in Kenya. It seemed like any other African adventure for the post-colonial white youth. Of course, I did not tell Eve this when I first met her in Eliot House—it is rude to be honest with strangers. What I did tell Eve was that she could stay with my family if she wanted. In Kenyan culture, visitors bring blessings.

I arrived in Nairobi a few days before Eve and was excited to meet her in Kisumu, where she would be staying with my Aunt Rose. From there, we planned to travel together to Nyabera. I've always enjoyed visiting the lakeside city of Kisumu. Maybe it is because Mr. Ndhiwa, my geography teacher, told us that Kisumu's Lake Victoria was the second largest fresh-water lake in the world after Lake Superior in America. We couldn't believe it. Our Lake Victoria was number two in the world!

On my way to Kisumu, I got a call from Aunt Rose, almost in a state of panic. She'd just learned that Eve was a vegetarian. How was she going to feed a vegetarian? Did Eve eat chicken? No. Did she eat fish? Surely, everyone must love the fresh fish of Lake Victoria. No, Eve did not eat fish. Eve only ate vegetables. How tragic. How would Aunt Rose feed her sensitive white stomach on only kale and beans?

# Eve

## Kisumu, Kenya

### JANUARY 2019

I had been awake for a little while when I got a message from Tom. He was almost here. No one else was awake, so I crept downstairs, padded barefoot across the hard dirt of Aunt Rose's yard, and gently unlocked her green metal gate. It sent a *clang* into the stillness. I leaned out and peered down the road.

There was Tom. He was still a block or two away, the only one out at this hour. The dawn air drifted hazily between us, the only noise the chatter of chickens. I waved.

His walk was a little stilted. As he got closer, I realized he looked the same as the last time I'd seen him; he might have even been wearing the same too-short-sleeved shirt. All at once, his arrival felt like a contortion of time and space—like a joke made late at night that turned real by accident.

"Eeeve Driver," Tom said as he approached, drawing out the single syllable of my first name. It was the same greeting as last time: a bit more playful, but still not warm. I laughed anyway and reached for a hug.

Once inside, Tom sank deeply into Aunt Rose's couch. He said he'd barely slept on his bumpy overnight bus ride from Nairobi, and I could see a part of him wanted to drift off then and there. Instead, he was about to turn around and take me on a four-hour bus ride to his home village, where we'd made plans to spend the weekend. I tried not to act as chipper as I felt; the poor guy needed some tea first, maybe a shower.

Aunt Rose heard us talking quietly and came in, greeting Tom with a formality I didn't expect and earning a deference I didn't recognize. Then she ducked into the kitchen to prepare tea and breakfast, just as she had each morning for the week I'd been with her.

When she left, so did the manners. Tom studied me with a weary and amused smile, seeming to sense that I perched on his aunt's wooden stool with an air of un-belonging. I could tell he was taking pleasure in my disorientation, like it was a joke I wasn't in on. The rest of my fellow researchers had booked a safari for the weekend, but I opted out of it; I was more interested in learning what Tom's idea of adventure entailed. When breakfast was ready, we ate quickly and set off.

In the days before I'd left for Kenya, Oliver told me more about Tom: the clean energy startup, the awards, the TED talk. "Tom has a lot of wisdom," he had said, and I was sure he did. Tom was the stuff of suburban college applicants' nightmares—the kind of hero that guidance counselors reassured us didn't actually exist, as they convinced us we could write a moving college essay even if our greatest hardship had been the SATs.

I also had questions. There was something about the shiny-on-paper types I'd met at college that made me skeptical. On top of that, my ecocriticism classes left me cringing at the many companies marketing themselves as "green," as it seemed most were full of at least a little bit of shit.

As we walked to the bus station, I asked Tom about the "green" in his company, GreenChar. I tried to listen closely. Of all the things I nerded out about, business models had never been one of them. Additionally, up to that point, my perspective on business was mainly defined by the adage, "people over profit," and I had the sense it was usually one or the other.

He explained that they had turned sugarcane waste into fuel for cooking. His hometown was mostly sugarcane farmers, he said, and they sold their crops to a processing plant nearby. The plant turned the green heaps of sugarcane into the sugar we know, then sold Tom and his co-founder the leftover parts of the cane. The sugarcane fuel they produced was a substitute for charcoal and helped reduce deforestation. I didn't get the connection, so Tom told me about the thousands of acres of trees that are cut down every year in Kenya so the wood can be burned into the black coal used in stoves. Burning the sugarcane waste, which they processed into little squares called briquettes, was smokeless. It was also cheaper.

As we reached the main street, we were interrupted by a van pulling up on the corner, blasting a little 9 a.m. club music. It pulsed louder when its doors opened, releasing a rash air of festivity. This was a *matatu*, the classic public transport here. Two older women climbed stiffly on board, unfazed, as the driver pulled back onto the street before the doors had even closed behind them. As the raucous music faded, the others on the corner went about their waiting or walking with a surreal indifference. By the time I turned back to Tom, he'd flagged down two *boda-bodas,* and a man in a vest was handing me a helmet.

Kenya's boda-bodas are motorbike taxis that flit through traffic with a finesse I'd been admiring since I arrived. I took the helmet with a self-satisfied flourish; as I put it on, I shot a look at Tom, who had clearly been prepared to mock me if I refused. These things were not the safest, and I'd been told by others never to ride one. After I slung my leg over, I spared a confused glance Tom's way to see how he was holding on. My instinct was to grab the driver's waist as I'd done with friends on a trip to Thailand, but something told me that was not the move. I spotted the crossbar Tom was holding just in time to avoid humiliation.

We made eye contact as his driver pulled abruptly onto the road. Over his shoulder, he shouted something to the effect of "See you there!"—presumably referring to the bus station, but knowing full well I didn't know where that was or what to do if the guy didn't take me there. It was going to be exhausting if he kept this up: milking his upper hand, making me feel an unrelenting pressure to be less of a white girl than he expected. His smugness made me feel ashamed of both my obliviousness and the fact I'd opted into it by following my frivolous urge to simply *go* places—to impose myself where I didn't belong, to flounder.

My driver waited two, then five seconds, probably for a break in the traffic. But my stomach flipped; if we lost Tom, I was frankly toast. Finally, my driver hit the gas. And boy, was it a rush, riding on that thing: my hair whipping against my face in a grand cliché of freedom, the matatus looking bulky and lame as we passed them on either side. Then my driver really stepped on it, maybe feeling obliged to catch us up. We sailed past another boda-boda, then another, until I recognized Tom's gray backpack getting nearer to my right.

"Yeehaw!" I shouted to him. Surprised, he craned his neck around and shouted something I couldn't hear as we sped past. A few moments later, he was gaining on us. I could see in the corner of my eye that his hand was outstretched. I turned around just the tiniest bit and saw it held an iPhone—that he was filming me while holding on with a single, cheeky hand.

---

# Tom

## Awendo, Kenya
### JANUARY

To succeed in a Kenyan bus station, one must become familiar with matatu culture. The matatu world operates with its own peculiar set of rules. The first step is to identify the brokers who sell the tickets—not always an easy feat as men fiercely compete to herd passengers aboard. In this, one has to be careful as the brokers will employ every trick in the book, like shouting "one more passenger"—a line as deceitful as it is effective. Then, there are the *makanga*—or as the Brits used to call them, "turn-boys"—whose sole job is to collect fares and fill every seat at each stop.

I looked over at Eve. I wondered if she was overwhelmed by it all: the hawkers pushing an array of snacks from lollipops to bananas, the cacophony of shouts and honks, the sizzle of roasting meat. In the thicket of brokers, I found the one for Awendo and haggled down the price of our tickets with Eve right behind me, following me as if afraid to get lost. One must always haggle ticket prices; there are different prices for different people, and if you are white, you must pay a premium—a sort of white tax.

The bus ride was the first time Eve and I spent more than thirty minutes together. We talked about international development and her work in Kisumu. What struck me about Eve was the resonance in her voice, a timbre tinged with an unmistakable conviction. At times, I thought perhaps her self-assuredness was a smokescreen for superficiality, a convenient mask for a lack of substance. But she seemed informed on the topic, and rather than absorb my skepticism, she challenged it, presenting new perspectives, questioning assumptions, and summoning evidence to bolster her points. I could see why she was majoring in social studies.

It was nearly 3 p.m. when our matatu rumbled to a halt beside the Indian mini-market in Awendo. As we stepped into the intense midday sun, I wasn't sure which was worse: the sweltering heat that now enveloped us or the insidious dust that had seeped into the vehicle, caking us with each jolt and bump on the journey from Kisumu. Still, I was happy to be back in Awendo. Home is always home. And Eve's smile suggested she was also happy to be there. Maybe it was the joy of finally stretching her legs or the giddiness that comes from the anticipation of new experiences.

Around us, boda-boda drivers jostled themselves into position, jockeying to become the "*mzungu*-carrier," or the bearer of the white woman. A familiar face sped to the forefront—it was Ouma, a glow radiating from his fat cheeks. Ouma and I grew up together, and in Awendo, kinship holds more currency than coin. His face shone with the pride of a rooster who had won a hen. But just then, my second cousin Owino pulled up in my mother's trusty gray Toyota Noah. Next time, *Ja-imbo*, next time.

Eve and I settled into the van's seats as Owino drove from the town center, soon easing into the slow rhythm of Awendo's roads. I wasn't sure what I could show Eve on this drive. Unlike Boston's unmistakable tourist attractions, Awendo's are less obvious, though still unique—rich in history and earthy texture. Awendo lies some 1,500 meters above sea level, its landscape a tapestry of small green hills that slope gently toward the River Sare, which bisects the town. The air here is scented with a blend of moisture and earth, thanks to the two distinct rainy seasons. The rain soaks the ground, creating a loamy, fertile soil for crops like sugarcane, tobacco, and maize. While the town's population is roughly 13,000 in its core, it's said that about 90,000 people live in the surrounding areas, many of whom are bound to the land and to one another, their lives and fates intertwined with the town's lifeblood—the sugarcane industry.

There was nothing in Awendo but land and greenery until South Nyanza Sugar Company set up shop in the sixties. Christened "Sony Sugar," the company became a magnet that drew people from all walks of life to Awendo. From the executives who handled the business side and engineers who tended the roaring engines and boilers, to the laborers needed for all sundry tasks and the truck drivers who delivered the sugarcane to the mill and the crystal sweetness to the markets, these people became the people of Awendo.

If I really wanted to show Eve this Awendo, my Awendo, I could have. But I chose not to. I was not going to let a white girl I barely knew (but was beginning to like) into my dusty, rusty world. That would have been naïve, too trusting. I did not want to show Eve Awendo's Centa, with its small, brick shops painted in peeling Safaricom green, or Sare—home of Awendo's so-called middle class—with its two-bedroom stone houses topped with red-painted roofs that Mama could only dream of living in. I was scared, and I was embarrassed. I couldn't introduce Eve to JiwDendi—which literally means "strengthen your body"—a dense slum of mud and tin houses huddled too close to a reeking, open sewer, a fact that does not seem to bother the patrons of the liquor dens serving *chang'aa*. If I had shown Eve JiwDendi, if I had shown her *my* Awendo, I would have faced my six-year-old self lying on the floor, on a mattress too thin to be called a mattress, my nose bleeding for hours, my head throbbing, my only resource the damp cloth that Baba placed on my forehead as he prayed over me.

Little had changed in Awendo. The road still meandered through the sprawling greenery of sugarcane fields, punctuated here and there by maize farms. Boda-bodas continued to bully the hapless cyclists and pedestrians sharing the road, and sugarcane tractors—massive and broad, with bellies full of freshly cut cane—still moved at a lumbering pace, almost wobbling under the weight of their cargo. When I was young, my little brother Benny and I seized upon this wobbling as an opportunity. We'd chase after the tractors, grasping for a dangling stalk of sugarcane. It was a mighty struggle, David wrestling Goliath. Sometimes, we'd succeed; when we did, we'd bite right into the uncleaned, untrimmed, and unpeeled stem.

Our van turned right onto a muddy murram road, jostling me back to the present. The lush greenery began to give way as we wobbled over bumps and potholes along a road so narrow the van's edges seemed to kiss the sugarcane leaves on either side. We were home.

# Eve

## Nyabera, Kenya
### JANUARY

Tom's mom must have heard the van's doors shut because she was waiting for us in the doorway as we made our way up the lawn. His dad soon appeared behind her. We said our hellos, and then, after the briefest of pauses, his parents began to sing.

I stood there and smiled, but in truth, I was reeling. On the way there, Tom and I had been crunched in the back corner of the van, our faces inches apart. He'd stared me straight in the eyes while explaining he wanted all international development efforts out of Africa—they were all versions of neocolonialism, including the work I'd been doing in Kisumu. "What we need is venture capital," he'd said. I had listened and nodded, though I'd been inclined to jump out the window. Despite bristling at what felt like a flippant indifference to the rampant gender violence in his country—which was on another scale compared to what I'd learned about in the workshops I'd hosted at school—I dropped it after several pointless back-and-forths. His anger was scalding. I didn't know the first thing about venture capital, but I knew it was not what I was there to offer. I pressed him on why he believed American influence was less neocolonial when it was motivated by profit—he responded something about bloating the local market economy and destabilizing it, as foreign impact dollars out-competed local businesses—but he clearly knew better than I did. By the end of the ride, I felt ready to head back to campus. Instead, I was meeting his parents.

As we were serenaded in the doorway, I wondered again why Tom had even invited me here. The only reason I'd come in the first place was because he'd offered to host me, which I assumed meant he wanted me here. Apparently, I'd been mistaken. I stole a glance in his direction. Who was this guy? Thinking back to the way he had flat-out dismissed the value of global women's empowerment, I began to feel something like anger rising up again.

But suddenly, his father met my gaze as he opened his chest and belted out a baritone, hymn-like melody. (Now I knew where Tom got his knack for jarring eye contact.) Then Tom's mom joined in with a warm alto, and everything softened. Then, it softened more. Then crescendoed. Tom's mom was all brightness. I could feel the words' religiosity reverberating in my body, could tell that God was being thanked for my arrival. I clasped my hands behind my back. Then I reclasped them upfront, unsure how to behave like someone worth singing for. All the while, I was experiencing a surreal type of whiplash. I'd never felt less—and then more thoroughly—welcomed.

Later, as I sat on my bed, I thought about what Oliver had said about Tom having a lot of "wisdom." It felt like such a cryptic thing to have said, and now here I was, thousands of miles from anywhere I could navigate without him. I grabbed my book and went out to the stoop. Staring at words always calms me down, even when I can't get myself to read them. After a while, Tom's father found me there and offered to give me a tour of his farm. The heat was subsiding, the shadows lengthening. Grateful, I accepted the invitation.

As we walked, I asked him what he was usually up to at this hour. He might be jogging, he told me; he would often go for long evening runs around his land, maybe down the road and then back around. I then asked him why he had decided to grow passion fruit, which Tom's mom had juiced and served us earlier. His eyes lit up. "That's a good story," he said.

We were nearing the edge of his property, and he pointed toward the east, where fields stretched on for miles. It was all sugarcane, he said. The county's crop. But he'd gotten tired of being swindled by the sugar conglomerate, which took wide margins from all the small farmers who had nowhere else to sell. So, he'd planted passion fruit. It thrived in the same kind of soil as sugar, so it worked well on his land. The fruit grew on vines that he wove through wooden lattices, and I was reminded of agroforestry. Of how growing trees and shrubs alongside crops can help combat climate change—as the trees absorb more carbon than crops alone while also improving soil health.

But Tom's dad didn't mention climate change. When I asked him about it, he told me that the climate would soon change from the heat of high summer. I'd forgotten that this was what the language of "climate change" meant to many people outside the university setting I was used to. He showed me that he was growing both the purple fruits and the sweet yellow ones. I hadn't known there were two types, and until that day, I'd never tasted either.

Tom's dad told me that God had blessed his crop of passion fruit and that it had made him good money. After he learned the plant's ways, he'd helped his neighbors get into the business. He lent some of them money and taught them what the plant liked and didn't like, and God blessed their crops, too. No longer beholden to the sugarcane industry, a small but mighty cohort had been set free by this fruit. I told him that I'd just finished reading a book called *Sweetness and Power*, which traces the way sugar went from being a raw material extracted from colonies and sold to a small slice of Europe's elite to a product consumed in excess by developed countries' lower classes, causing obesity epidemics while wealthier folks ate salad. He grinned, but his eyes kept moving to somewhere behind me, as though he was listening to the sound of my voice but not what I was saying. I shut up and let us fall gently into silence.

We walked until the sun began to leaf through the green cane on the horizon. Tom's dad asked me if I had ever grown anything, and I told him about my vegetable garden. He asked what I had grown, and for whatever reason, I told him a story about this one Earth Day when my entire fourth-grade class had been given tree saplings. I'd named mine Athena and planted her beside my garden. But a week later, I'd come down to water everyone and found her gone. And then I remembered the sharp humming I'd heard earlier that day: the weed wacker. Somberly, I told my poor dad what he had done, which, of course, he hadn't meant to—Athena looked suspiciously weed-like so early in her development. I forgave him.

Because Tom's dad listened so well, I told him about the pain I'd felt that day. The way trees have always felt so sacred to me. For the first time, not a shred of me cared if it sounded whimsical.

He asked me if I believed in God. I told him I did. But I explained that while church had been an important part of my childhood, Harvard was a pretty secular place, and that I wondered if I'd be more religious if I were surrounded by religious people.

"I hate when they call us 'religious people,'" he replied. "We all live here in the Kingdom of God." I guessed it made sense: like being called an "oxygen person" when you know it's what we all breathe. It reminded me of the frustration I sometimes felt when people referred to my focus on climate change as an "interest," as if it was more similar to knitting than a meteor on a collision course with Earth. I was fascinated by this man and his evangelism and his subversive, godly fruits.

# Tom

## Nyabera, Kenya
### JANUARY

That first night in Nyabera was peaceful. We feasted on wet-fried chicken in a tomato and onion sauce, chapatis, and rice. My mum even managed to pull together a vegetarian meal for Eve with kale, beans, and plenty of eggs. I'd forgotten how much I missed the freshness of home-cooked meals—we raised the hens we fried, grew the kale we steamed, and harvested the passion fruits we squeezed. At Harvard, I'd learned that they call this "farm-to-table."

Eve seemed to quickly form a bond with Baba. That was not surprising. Baba is a naturally curious conversationalist. He is also a devout man; many years ago, he'd answered when Jesus knocked on his soul's door. His conversion to Christianity had been transformative. It is said that many were shocked. Baba, after all, had something of a reputation across Awendo. He'd even served some time. But he had grown in the Lord and found his true calling: becoming a pastor and shepherding his own flock at the Jesus the King Worship Ministries.

I was raised in the shadow of Baba's pastoral journey. Thursday evenings were for the "house-visit" fellowships. Sometimes, only a couple of people would come; other times, the crowd would spill from our mud house into the yard. We would sing and dance. The mood would then shift to a somber reverence during the sharing of the Word. Faces would go expressionless, buttocks would be stuck to seats, and bodies would break into fervent prayer. Some would kneel, lifting their arms to the heavens; others would weep. Occasionally, Baba would lay hands on them, becoming a conduit channeling divine blessings from Heaven to Earth. I might not have understood all that was said, but I understood that it was deep and poignant. Afterward, we'd have tea and snacks—hot, milky tea laced with sugar and scrumptious red mini-muffins that Baba baked in a makeshift mud oven. When Nyabera became too small for the flock, we moved into a church in Awendo. We were the church, and the church was us. We cleaned, arranged seats, ushered people in, attended Sunday School, and joined the praise and worship team.

Around my ninth or tenth birthday, Benny and I received tracksuits from Baba—a highlight of my early years, perhaps only rivaled by the bike we got the following Christmas. These tracksuits were sacred. Mine was yellow, Benny's a greenish gray, and they weren't for jogging or PE class. They were our Sunday best, donned for special or open-air church services where we played our tambourines and danced along the roadside or in the Awendo market. My favorite song was "Hakuna Mungu Kama Wewe Yahweh!" When the lead vocalist would belt it out, I'd join in with impassioned "ahs" out of tune but full of joy. Benny and I would put one foot forward, raise an arm, and twirl in unison, proclaiming God's undeniable truth.

As I got older, I attempted to learn the keyboard. And when our regular keyboardist moved from Awendo, Baba called upon my eleven-year-old self to lead the praise and worship services. Sometimes, I felt that I would crumble under the weight of expectations, but Baba told me that in the Kingdom of God, only the effort mattered. For God peered deep into our hearts, rewarding only our earnest endeavors.

Faith was the cornerstone of our family, the glue that held us together despite all odds. I wondered what Eve would make of this.

On our second day together, I decided to show Eve around Nyabera, my Nyabera. Our first stop was St. Benedict's, where I'd gone to school from ages ten to fourteen. The school was on holiday when we arrived; the frenetic energy of my school days was replaced by quiet. The principal, Mr. Oguta, was in his office, which still sat at the intersection of a verandah that doubled as an assembly ground every morning. I was struck by the familiarity of it all. The same light-brown desk and wooden chair beside the trophy-laden cabinet. The long table in the center of the room, its chairs neatly arranged like attendees at a meeting. The handwritten manila poster that showcased the mean test scores of each graduating class and the bolded names of those who had excelled in the Kenya Certificate of Primary Education (KCPE) exams. But there was something new, a fresh addition that hung alongside these testaments to academic achievement. A blue plastic plaque inscribed with white serif letters that read: God listens.

I looked at Eve as her eyes darted around the room, absorbing every detail. I wondered how she would synthesize this part of my past. This room was not just an office; it was a sanctuary, a microcosm of the ethos and achievements of St. Benedict's, presided over by a man who had chosen to invest his energy in shaping young lives like mine.

Mr. Oguta was my Kiswahili teacher. I had been taken aback by his charisma and enthusiasm for the subject. Many headmasters don't enjoy teaching, but Mr. Oguta taught with such vigor that his lessons sometimes resembled a Baptist church revival service. But teaching Kiswahili was Mr. Oguta's secondary goal; his first was ensuring all forty-one of us passed our KCPE exams. During the first week of Class Eight, he walked into our classroom and declared that no student would fail the exams due to poor handwriting. Not on his watch. He took a one-meter wooden ruler, drew straight lines across the board, and meticulously wrote the alphabet from *Aa* to *Zz*. That was the exemplar, and from then on, we were all to write as neatly and meticulously as Mr. Joseph Oguta himself.

Soon after, Mr. Oguta moved on to phase two of his master plan: ensuring we each scored at least a 70 percent in all subjects. The first item on the agenda was "Dawn Sums." Every morning, at 5 a.m., before the rooster could even crow, we'd rise and make our way to the classroom where Mr. Milungo waited with a paraffin lamp in his left hand and chalk in his right. With deliberate care, he would write twenty math problems on the board. We were to copy and solve each problem correctly. Failure to do so resulted in three strong strokes from a cane and our name forwarded to Mr. Oguta for further action.

Standing there with Eve and Mr. Oguta, I looked around the classroom where I spent so much of my youth. Peeling paint revealed layers of faded colors on the walls. Wooden desks—each a unique spectacle of splinters and carved initials—sagged and tilted on uneven legs. The air was a heavy blend of mildew and old books.

The more things change, the more they stay the same.

---

# Eve

## Nyabera, Kenya
### JANUARY

It had been many years since Tom and Mr. Oguta had seen each other, and I sat and listened as the two caught up. Harvard: What was it like? America: What did Tom think of it? They reminisced about Tom's years in Awendo and how overjoyed they had been when Tom was admitted to one of the country's elite public boarding schools.

At first, the tone was light-hearted. But after a pause—and in the kind of voice reserved for grand, long-awaited unveilings—Mr. Oguta announced that he had known all along that Tom would be admitted. He had watched Tom pore over his algebra books, had pushed him harder than any other student he had ever had. He had known it was Tom's destiny; God had let him know years in advance.

As I watched Tom take this in, a humble gratitude seemed to overcome him. When he finally spoke, his voice was so gentle, so childlike. His eyes did not water, but I caught the faintest tremble move across his face, as if he could barely breathe with the weight, the joy, of all he owed this man in front of him. I wanted to reach over and put my hand on his shoulder or something, an urge I quickly remembered was wildly out of step with our current rapport—but in that moment, everything I felt toward him seemed to reset, as though I were meeting him again for the first time. I marveled at how many versions of Tom existed and how many I had already gotten to meet.

As we were leaving, Mr. Oguta made it clear that guiding Tom to success had been the crowning achievement of not just his career but his life; so rarely do we get the chance to know God's will and then be pivotal in enacting it. I got the chills. I did not know Tom's religious beliefs, but now I wanted to. There were a lot of things about him that I wanted to know.

———

Later that afternoon, we pulled into a parking lot tucked behind a row of storefronts. Tom said he would be a failure if he let me come all the way to Awendo only to leave without trying the local beer. Hopping out of the van, I was surprised to see the bar decorated with green turf and string lights; the place looked almost like any craft brewery back home. We sat down at a white plastic table and ordered two Tuskers.

We sipped our beers slowly. We had two more days together.

"So, what's the plan for tomorrow?" I asked after a sip. Tom's face looked tired at my question.

"Are you already bored by Awendo?"

"No!" I said, "I was just wondering." After a moment, I suggested, "We could go for a hike or something."

He laughed. "You Americans and your hiking." He shook his head; he was always shaking his head at me.

"What's wrong with hiking?" I asked.

"And the camping, too," he added.

"What's wrong with camping?!" I was laughing now, pretending to be indignant, though curious about where he was going with this.

"You all are so comfortable that you think it's fun to go into the woods and make extra work for yourselves."

"I guess so," I replied. "We just don't really think of hiking as 'work.'"

"You want to feel courageous, so you go put up tents in the forest."

"Because it's fun! You can see the stars."

"And then after one night, you've had enough, so you go back to your running water and your lights, and you Instagram *allll* about it."

There was an edge in his voice now, but he had a point. I'd read about *intersectional environmentalism*, the idea that the systems oppressing marginalized communities and the Earth are interconnected and that identities like race, class, and gender shape how we relate to the natural world. But I felt like he was being too snide for me to let him off that easily.

"It's not about a 'lower' standard of living," I replied. "It's like a trade: you're giving up the comforts of a nice house for all the beauty and ambiance of a forest."

"Right, so it's only fun if you have those comforts to give up in the first place."

"Which more than half the world *does* have, and it's led those societies to be disconnected from nature in a way that's unhealthy." An edge had crept into my voice now, too.

"So, you sleep in a tent in order to save the planet?" Tom asked in genuine contempt. It stung.

I was startled when, just then, a young man tapped Tom on the shoulder; I hadn't noticed him walking toward us across the green.

"Ian," Tom said, breaking into a smile.

Ian must have caught the tail end of our conversation. He shot Tom a sly smile that seemed to ask if he was interrupting. Tom and I rose to our feet and greeted him.

Ian was Tom's cofounder. He had come by to catch up.

Tom and I hadn't spoken much about GreenChar since that first morning at his aunt's house. When Ian and Tom's chatter turned to the company, I took the opportunity to ask some more questions.

"So, you just use the part of the sugarcane that isn't sugar?" I asked. "And do you have to pay for it?"

Ian said of course they did; everyone was trying to make a buck. He told me more about the sugar company they bought it from. I was intrigued by how GreenChar seemed to subvert neocolonialism and fossil fuels simultaneously. Suddenly, the idea that "capitalism" could be talked about as if it were a single thing seemed absurd. Back at school, it felt like we'd been conflating Western corporate capitalism with all these other modes—as if capitalism operated the same way around the world. Here, there were the foreign-run companies and the local: the ones whose only aspirations were profit and those designed with sustainability at their core. The sugar industry continued to leave places like Awendo—and people like Tom's father—at the mercy of foreign-owned corporations who kept all the profit. By buying and creating value from the sugar company's waste, Tom and Ian had found a way to start building a new, local economy on top of and beyond the old one.

Halfway through my Tusker, the whole thing was starting to strike me as brilliant. My stomach dropped as I felt myself begin to hurtle down from the ivory tower that had paid for me to come here. It felt almost sickening, like the way it feels to fall inside a dream. Yet I felt the urge to pump my arms, to fall faster—back down to Earth before anyone else could see that I'd ever been so far up there in the first place.

As the waitress brought Ian his beer, he turned to tell Tom about his new compressor and his latest round of fundraising.

I zoned out. Like before, business terminology began to fly over my head as if it were in Luo, the language of Tom's tribe. I think some of it was.

I perked up when I heard Ian mention Boulder.

"Boulder, Colorado?" I asked. They turned to me like they'd forgotten I was there.

"Yeah, Colorado." Ian was starting to peg me as a space cadet.

"And sorry, what was it you were doing there?"

"I was at a startup incubator focused on climate and clean energy," he replied.

I nodded. They continued. I'd never been to Boulder, but among the American outdoorsy, it was rumored to be a sort of utopia. I had friends and family who'd gone to college out there, who seemed to have spent four blissful years smoking weed and strumming folk songs on guitars. *Of course they would have clean energy incubators out there*, I thought. And whatever it was that Tom seemed to have against us Americans, Boulderites seemed like just the kind of crowd that would want to help Ian out.

After saying goodbye, Tom and I drove the old silver van back down the dark, winding road to Nyabera. There were no streetlights, and as far as I could tell, there was no moon. Where there had been fields of sugarcane, there was now a thick blackness, broken only by our two feeble headlights.

Suddenly, from around a bend came a roar and burst of light. My stomach flipped as what looked like a rogue and oversized train hurtled toward us from the other direction. There wasn't a shred of doubt in my mind that it was going to hit us. I squealed and closed my eyes. When I opened them, Tom was laughing, really laughing, with his whole face and belly. But it no longer felt snide. It might have been almost affectionate.

"I forgot to tell you about the one-eyed monsters," he said.

"The what?" I said, now laughing too—my heartbeat starting to steady.

"They're the trucks that carry the sugarcane. Big, with just one headlight."

"That seems like a major design flaw," I said.

"Don't worry," Tom said. "The road is always wide enough." Somehow, I believed him.

We pulled back onto Tom's lawn. The faint glow of a TV shone through the window as we crossed the short grass. It was the end of one of those days that feels like several. Between meeting Mr. Oguta and Ian, it was as though we'd retraced Tom's whole life.

Inside, his parents were eating. The table was lit with a lantern, which—like the TV—was solar-powered. Here, solar was the only way to get electricity. I'd never seen one of these lanterns before, and Tom's father proudly showed off the battery that could be taken out and recharged on sunny days. It glowed like blue candlelight.

# Tom

## Nyabera, Kenya

JANUARY

There are certain constants about Ian, like the wide grin on his face or the fact that he always wears a black T-shirt and black denim jeans. We met in February 2010 when I moved from Awendo to Kikuyu Town—on the outskirts of Nairobi—for boarding school. At first, I'd taken him to be hardworking (after all, he had ranked eighth in the entire country in our KCPE exams), but Ian was anything but a model student. He was perennially asleep in class, seldom completed his homework, and was a fixture on Mr. Kinyanjui's notorious list of noisemakers. It was easy to write Ian off.

What eventually drew me to him was his street-smart ingenuity, like his weekend escapades to the nearby Kikuyu Town Center. School rules allowed us only to leave campus on Saturday and Sunday afternoons. Ian would use this time to buy lollipops, then wait until Wednesday—when everyone's stash had run out—to sell them at thrice the normal price.

Our camaraderie began when we started doing science projects together in Form 2D. Our first was a home science experiment aimed at accelerating the ripening of bananas. By the following year, we realized we had a shared entrepreneurial spirit and launched Kenya Teen Connect, an app where high school students could post photos of themselves. It failed within a week. Then, we conceptualized SkyMed, a cloud-based patient medical record storage. But it also never took off. While disappointing, these lessons only made us more resilient and persuasive. In the early days of what would become GreenChar, we managed to convince the notoriously stubborn Mr. Mutali to allow us to use the school farm for our experiments (though he would later get cold feet when it became apparent that we were absconding one too many classes). Still, we remained convinced that GreenChar could work. We were seventeen and disenchanted with the conventional "system." Instead, we vowed to blaze our own trails, to craft our own realities. We made a pact to forego college.

When we graduated from high school, we officially founded GreenChar beneath the shade of a mango tree in Nyabera. Baba was incredibly supportive. With Baba's help, along with the funding from Jacob and Innovate Kenya, we designed a compact kiln system to turn sawdust and sugarcane waste into clean-burning fuel. We hired a *fundi* to build the kiln based on our desired specifications—bringing our design to life. And Nyagideya, a local woman who lived nearby, became our first employee. She wore a smile every single day, diligent in her work beneath the inadequate shade of that mango tree in Nyabera.

Within a year, we raised $200,000 from American investors and built a factory. One of our funders was Echoing Green, an American organization whose mission is to "discover emerging social entrepreneurs and invest deeply in the growth of their ideas and leadership." We eventually moved GreenChar's headquarters to Nairobi with the aim of selling to low-income homes in Kibera, but after eighteen months, that move would get us into trouble with al-Shabaab.

Ian and I both left GreenChar in 2016 and made our way to the US—I went to Boston, and he went to Boulder. We left the company in the care of a white American woman who'd moved to Nairobi after marrying a Kenyan. She had worked as a manager for a solar company in Brooklyn, where she'd launched a new social venture that made solar more accessible to diverse communities and generated at least $1.5 million in signed contracts. She'd also worked at GreenChar as the Head of Operations for a year. When she jumped ship and launched her own competing business within the first year of our absence, Ian flew home to stabilize the situation. GreenChar was, in every sense, on its last legs. But Ian had a knack for reviving dying embers.

———

That evening, as Eve and I drove back to Nyabera, I imagined that Eve and I were connected by the very same things that had connected Ian and me: a natural curiosity, a shared sense of adventure, and an almost innate inclination to reimagine our worlds as they could be rather than just accepting them as they were. We were all dreamers in our right—each from different corners of the world, yet united by the desire to understand and shape our place in the universe.

---

# Eve

## Nyabera, Kenya
### JANUARY

During my visit, I quickly learned that Mrs. Osborn spent most of her time in the kitchen: kneeling, washing greens, hanging her blackened pots above the charcoals. Up early the next morning, I went to find her to see if I could help. She was making mandazis. As she began showing me how to make the dough, it became clear that my "help" was more trouble than it was worth, but she didn't seem to mind. We kneeled together, the four round bulbs of our knees in a row beside the hearth. She showed me how to stoke the coals that gleamed blue. Her arms looked strong next to my spaghetti ones.

Growing up, I always liked cooking outside more than in the kitchen. Inside, I felt haunted by the specter of traditional gender roles. But around a campfire, I felt intrepid. When I knelt over the flames next to Tom's mom, it felt cozy and familiar—like something I'd done once or twice a year for as long as I could remember, a thing I did because it made me feel more free, more wild.

Yet alongside that feeling crept the sting of Tom's words from the day before, making that parallel feel a little ridiculous. I was still thinking about what Tom had said—about how people like me relish the novelty inherent in lifestyles like this, lifestyles that people like his mother live out of necessity. As the flames began to lick the bottom of the pan, the same one she cooked with every day, I realized I could not have explained how I was feeling to her even if we shared the same language. Instead of talking, we just kept looking at each other and laughing. Her laugh came from somewhere deep, like she was laughing at all of life and not just at whatever was happening here. Her taste for the absurd seemed a lot like Tom's.

As we kneaded the dough and she showed me how to form the shape of the mandazis, my knees—still folded underneath me—began to stiffen, and I switched to a gangly cross-legged. She laughed at me warmly as we coaxed the flames higher. Fire, it turns out, works about the same everywhere—the same laws of physics, the same hypnotic flicker.

As the dough began sizzling, I noticed a haze forming. The kitchen seemed to shrink as the flames grew, kicking off a smoke that did not rise obediently up the chimney but hung in the quiet air between us. The only light, which came in through the open doorway to the yard where chickens pecked around freely, illuminated the smoke enough that we could see it swirl, slow and counterclockwise. It tasted nostalgic as I breathed it in.

When he'd first told me about GreenChar, Tom had mentioned air pollution. He hadn't mentioned his mom. That part he'd shared with me later. He'd explain how breathing as much smoke as air, day in and day out, had led to respiratory infections that threatened to grow more serious—into some sort of lung disease or cancer. He'd share how this fear for his mother's lungs—and those of millions of women in sub-Saharan Africa—was what had turned GreenChar from a high-school pipe dream into something real and urgent. As we plated the food, I thought of the young girls I'd seen carrying water on their heads, of the studies I'd read showing that it was often women who were the first to feel the effects of a changing climate, who had their fingers most tenderly on the pulse of the planet as it tossed and turned.

———

After breakfast, Tom fired up the silver van, and we were back on the road. Despite his griping about the whole hiking enterprise, he'd run out of ideas. The drive to the trailhead took us through hot terrain that looked more like desert the further we drove: rocky and arid and flat enough that the "road" appeared as little more than some signage.

As we bantered and pointed out weirdly-shaped trees on the roadside, it was clear something had changed between us. The very fact that we were here, doing this, seemed to open the possibility that we could disagree and then get over it. The whole trip now had an irony to it that lightened us. It hit me that throughout all my earnest studies, all my questions about nature and culture, I had never laughed about them—I had never come close. Laughing had not seemed possible, but Tom's laughter was different; it was deeper. Somehow, without lowering any of the stakes, his laughter brought us back down to earth.

We pulled into the parking lot in a cloud of hot gray dust. This was the site of an old Luo community, with some of the ruins dating back hundreds of years. Tom and his family were members of the Luo tribe.

The guide stationed at the entry brought us toward a series of small mud homes with thatched roofs. Inside the first one, he looked at me and said, "This is where you will store the grain," then, "And this is where you will grind it to flour." Tom and I both lost it when the guide showed us the spot where I'd give birth to our baby; he had pegged us for newlyweds.

Next, he brought us up to a stone enclosure about the size of a football field that once held livestock. We had to walk up a long hill to get there, and I said something to Tom about finally getting our hike in. When he didn't reply, I looked over and saw he was winded. I almost laughed out loud.

The more I sat with them, the more I understood that Tom's feelings toward American "outdoors" culture were deeply real. He'd been getting at something so much bigger, relaying a broader alienation that helped explain why the vast majority of the Outing Club I was in back at school was still white and middle-class—and why, to many, "environmentalism" still implies caring about white people, then birds, then people of color, in that order.

In both Kenya and the United States, most outdoor recreation happens on land that was wrested from Indigenous people, and experiencing it often requires time and expensive equipment. Ultimately, the privileged get to feel like we're testing our complacency when we go into the mountains and create primal struggles for ourselves, only to return to work on Monday without ever reflecting on the systems of power that sustain us.

As I watched Tom clamber awkwardly up that grassy slope, all our tiffs began to strike me as so personal. For all his obvious wisdom, even Tom's loftiest takes on the world were just as shaped by his own individual strengths and weaknesses as everybody else's. This did not make them less true, but more.

When the tour was over, we made our way back down the hill to the parking lot. In the heavy heat, our guide had displayed ridiculous stamina. Both Tom and I were relieved to collapse back into the van and laughed freely about our guide's faith in my prospects as a Luo wife.

"I think I'm past the point in my life where I just want to explore," Tom said suddenly on the drive home, breaking the silence.

I turned to look at him. His face betrayed a rare earnestness.

"What makes you say that?" I asked.

"I am interested only in action," he replied.

"Hmm," I said.

We both turned back to our windows. I thought about this idea for a long time.

———

The next morning, over a breakfast of chapati, I learned that Tom had saved the best stop on our tour for last: the GreenChar factory.

Around mid-morning, the violence prevention program team I'd been working with pulled onto Tom's lawn, windswept and giddy after seeing all of the Big Five beasts. We'd arranged for them to pick me up in Awendo on the way back from their weekend safari; they wanted to see the factory, too.

Ian was there when we arrived. The space was bigger than I'd expected, with tall sheet metal walls and a large fence enclosing the yard. Ian told us that he'd ordered most of the materials from China. We followed him inside.

Now that he had a bigger audience, Ian fielded questions about the company as though presenting to a panel of investors. I could see why he and Tom had gotten funding. The pitch rolled off his tongue smoothly, the narrative of the whole venture coming off like a truly mouth-watering tale of human ingenuity.

And it *was* that, no doubt. But without the Tusker making everything rosier, I was back to wondering what was being left out. Reducing carbon emissions, protecting the health of Tom's mom and other vulnerable women, creating jobs, turning a profit—I felt sure there was no way it could all be possible. I'd been taught to mistrust such tidy storytelling. I'd recently read *Merchants of Doubt*, which details how a team of PR professionals hired by the tobacco industry paid pseudo-scientists at pseudo-think-tanks to suggest that the link between smoking and cancer was dubious. Having mastered these disinformation techniques, this same PR team was then employed by the oil and gas industry to do it all over again. The story left me reeling and made me wonder: if those kinds of shenanigans were possible—if a little charisma and hand-waving could invalidate the most rigorous of science, imperil entire island nations, and go unpunished—how could any company be trusted to tell its own story?

But I had run out of questions. I knew so little about business it was hard to know where to begin, how to spot the holes that were open for poking. So, I just listened.

Ian drew our attention to a massive chute in the center of the warehouse, angled down like a slide. This was where the sugarcane waste was pushed down and compressed, he explained. Now that they were selling to schools and other large institutions with big furnaces, they needed to manufacture massive blocks of fuel. A trace of glee escaped Ian's stoic demeanor as he climbed up to turn it on and show us how it worked. He reminded me of my older brother when he was nine, riding atop a tiny motorized green gator from Toys R Us yelling, "beep, beep, beep!" while I sat in my garden and led the carrot harvest by hand.

Ian fired up something that sounded hydraulic. At this point, he was way, way up there, looking superhuman, as though the massive hunk of metal beneath him was somehow an extension of his body. Given that the whole thing had been conceived and made real through his work, I imagined it probably felt that way. He shouted something I couldn't hear over the general grinding of the machinery.

I looked over at Tom, wondering if he missed being part of all this. There must have been so many things Ian had learned in the three years Tom had been a student—lessons that professors or books couldn't teach. Tom looked proud but a bit wistful as he watched Ian shut down the machine with cool expertise.

When we piled back into the van, it felt like I'd been away from the team for weeks. They told me about their adventures and asked me about mine, but I didn't know quite how to answer. Something about the past four days felt hard to narrate, as though simply listing the series of events would fall wildly short of the truth.

---

# Tom

## Nyabera, Kenya
### JANUARY

Since heading to college, I had deliberately distanced myself from Green-Char. But showing Eve around the old factory in Nyabera had done something—it breathed life into those three dormant years. As I rode the bus to Nairobi after spending the weekend with Eve, it hit me just how neatly I'd tucked GreenChar away.

I've always enjoyed the bus rides from Awendo to Nairobi. The first was when I was twelve, for my brother Micah's graduation from the police academy. The second was when I was fifteen, this time to attend boarding school in Kikuyu, a small town on the outskirts of the city. Then there were the many trips during the early GreenChar days, after we moved our headquarters to Ongata Rongai, one of the many emerging, dusty towns around Nairobi. Back in the day, Rongai was a dry outpost for Maasai nomads who would call it home for a few months before moving on when the drought began to bite. But as Nairobi expanded and the cost of city living soared, the emerging middle class began gravitating toward Rongai.

To get to Rongai, one took a ninety-minute matatu from Nairobi's Railway Station. Our GreenChar offices were just outside Rongai's town center in a three-story building adjacent to a street garage. The entrance was marked by a narrow trench filled with an assortment of industrial detritus—black oil, aged tires, stray metal pieces, murky water, and other liquid waste. Inside, we made do with what we had, partitioning the space with plywood to create two areas: one for the office and the other for storage.

We relocated to Rongai due to our new partnership with Envirofit, an American cookstove manufacturer. I first met their Country Director—a middle-aged white man—at their Nairobi warehouse. I was blown away by how much faith he had in me.

The story of Envirofit was intriguing. Funded primarily by Shell Oil, the company was founded in Colorado and successfully distributed $30 clean-burning cookstoves across Africa and South Asia. On its face, the value to consumers appeared compelling: Envirofit stoves reduced fuel consumption by 58 percent, reduced toxic emissions by 56 percent, and were two times as efficient as traditional cookstoves. If we were to combine their stoves with our clean-burning charcoal, we would have a winning combo, or so we thought.

At the time, I didn't consider how odd it was that Envirofit, a rising star in the nascent clean cooking movement, had entered a long-term partnership with Shell, a cornerstone of the fossil fuel industry. In fact, in 2007, Shell awarded Envirofit a $25 million grant to design and distribute ten million clean-burning cookstoves in developing countries. It was still financing Envirofit in 2014 when we set up in Rongai. Later, Eve would suggest that perhaps this was Shell's way of providing cover for the environmental damage they caused. But back then, I was just an ambitious eighteen-year-old. If Shell was willing to bankroll my dream, what else was there to say? We would bundle Envirofit's cookstoves with our clean-burning charcoal and tap into their existing distribution network.

As I made my way back to Nairobi, I thought of all this and more, reflecting on the bumps and missteps Ian and I had taken on the path to clean energy. Still, I hadn't told Eve everything. I hadn't told her what happened with al-Shabaab in Kibera or how Ian had picked up the ashes of GreenChar in my absence. I had only just met Eve, and what I had told her was enough.

# Eve

## Nairobi, Kenya
### JANUARY

One of the many things I'd told Tom about during our time together was my pants collection. I collected colorful, patterned pants, which I added to every time I visited a new country. By the time I got to Kenya, I had pairs from sixteen countries across five continents, all of which hung on a clothesline from my dorm room ceiling. Tom promised to help me find a Kenyan pair before I went home.

I spent the last day of my trip in Nairobi crashing with Tom at his brother's apartment. His brother was now the fourth member of Tom's family I'd been introduced to; it was the most family I'd met of any of my college friends.

In the morning, we took a taxi into the heart of the city. While Tom chatted with the driver in Swahili, I looked out the window, watching as skyscrapers began to rise over open-air markets. When we got out, I looked around and didn't see any pants.

"Are we going to an indoor mall?"

"First, we are going to the Supreme Court."

I laughed and looked at Tom with grateful disbelief. Last night, he'd commented on my T-shirt with a silhouette of Ruth Bader Ginsberg. He must have thought I'd be interested.

We walked over to the fence and looked at the building. We decided it was less imposing than America's: more of a place to accomplish essential business than some sort of monument to Truth and Justice. Tom told me a funny story about the making of the Kenyan Constitution.

Next, we poked our noses into a bookstore. As I watched Tom browse, his eyes lighting up when he showed me a book written by his favorite Kenyan poet, I began to realize that despite all his talk about learning more from the "School of Hard Knocks" than from any classroom, he was really a little bookworm at heart.

But the pants—it was already lunchtime, and we hadn't found any yet. We ducked inside a shopping center and were immediately overwhelmed with fabrics: red, green, orange, yellow, and some particularly flamboyant teals. I looked around. The instant I started stroking a pair of high-waisted slacks, a man poked his head around from behind the rack and asked if I wanted to try them on. Before I could reply, he was already taking them off the hanger. I ducked behind a curtain and slipped the pants on over my shorts.

"What do you think?"

Tom nodded.

"I'll take them," I told the man.

I bargained him down from $12 to $10 and called it a victory. Tom just stood to the side and grinned.

"What's next? Do you want a photo op of a giraffe licking your face? That is the white woman's favorite stop in Nairobi."

"I'm alright," I said.

Later, we went looking for dinner, which turned out to be no small feat for a vegetarian. Soon, Tom was marching right up to restaurant hosts and asking if there was any way they could just combine beans with *chapati* to make a makeshift vegetarian dish. Twice, the answer was no. But to my surprise, instead of seeming annoyed with me, Tom only became a more impassioned vegetarian ally—grumbling about the restaurants that wouldn't accommodate us.

When we finally found a place, they sat us on a roof deck, and we remembered how great cities are, letting you experience them on so many different planes. We talked about how the air up there felt thinner, cleaner. Tom asked if this was what it felt like to climb a mountain.

"Thanks for putting up with my vegetarianism," I said after we'd settled in. "I'm sorry to be such a pain."

I'd slowly begun to grasp why vegetarianism is so widely scoffed at here, especially for those who can't take any of their meals for granted. It must be bizarre and annoying to imagine the privilege one must enjoy to simply opt out of such a vital source of protein. Kenya also doesn't have the same problem with factory farming the US does, and meat is a sacred part of the culture, so it was hard to explain my rationale for opting out in the first place.

Tom grew suddenly stern, disappointed even.

"You apologize too much," he said. "Do what you think is right, and people will follow."

He got up to use the bathroom, and I sat stunned, trying to figure out when Tom had come to see me so thoroughly—when he'd become one of the people in my life invested in making me stronger.

Since it was my last night, we had planned to make it wild. Tom knew how much I love to dance and claimed he had some spots in mind downtown where he was "boys" with the DJ and could promise me a good time. But in the dimming light of his brother's living room, we could tell that the city was too quiet and we were too tired. So, we followed the cat out to the back patio and played with him until he grew bored of us. But we still hadn't grown bored of each other, so we sat up into the night, broaching new topics like cannabis spirituality and the directions of our ambiguous futures. I had no way of knowing how the neighborhood usually sounded, but the night's silence felt charged, as though a static energy was pulsing through the black, humid air. As we sat on the stoop, our words cut through it all—weighty and sharp.

The conversation turned to Harvard.

"Are you going to abandon me when we get back to campus?" Tom asked. I looked at him to try to read his expression, but as usual, it was an impenetrable blend of taunting and earnestness.

"Why would you think that?" I asked. It was a strange way of saying he wanted to stay friends.

"I don't know," he said.

We talked about our freshman years.

"I heard of you, actually," I told him.

"Is that right?"

"Yes, because of the Prince of Wakanda thing." I'd forgotten this until recently, but Tom had gone around telling people he was the Prince of Wakanda to see who would fall for it. "Kids were talking about you in the dining hall."

He laughed and then was silent. His mind seemed to be going back to that time and reprocessing.

"Was Harvard what you expected it would be?" I asked after a moment.

"Not really," he replied, his eyes snapping back into focus. "I kind of expected...since, you know, it's *Harvard*"—his voice did the whole scare-quotes thing—"everyone there would be trying to figure out how to save the world."

"And that's not what you found?"

"Not most people. It seems like most people there are just trying to get rich and get laid. Or maybe famous."

"I'm not going to abandon you," I said. But I realized that I meant it only after I had said it. We both knew that except for knowing Oliver, we ran in different circles; it was not a coincidence we hadn't met sooner. But in my three years, I'd never met anyone like him, anyone I had such a stubborn and compulsive urge to figure out. And despite or because of all the ways we grated against each other, some weird gravity seemed to draw us together, threatening to snap us. It felt as dramatic then as it feels today.

On the plane the next day, I tried to imagine how it must have felt for Tom to fly all the way to the US, expecting to find himself among the next generation of changemakers and join their ranks. Instead, he'd found that even at Harvard, and maybe everywhere, we were all just running around—barely getting our own shit together, let alone humanity's. What a sense of disorder that must have meant for him: a sense of hopelessness and, perhaps, also an unburdening.

The airplane rose quickly, making the setting sun sink faster, as though we were chasing the night, leaving those on the ground to manage the last hour of daylight without us. I pressed my face against my window's glass, wanting to feel its coolness as the city grew smaller. The people—now too small to watch—slipped back into their customary position of very far away from me.

In the days ahead, I knew I'd be back with my books. The real world would fade slightly, my distance vision worsening and making me squint to see the faces of those waving to me as I walked home from the library at dusk. I looked forward to all this; I had loved the start of school since kindergarten. And yet, as the engine that carried me spat thousands of tons of carbon into the sky, I felt for the first time like whatever divine faith I'd had in my coursework, in its promise to mold me into a person doing good in the world, had started to give out on me.

Watching Tom and Ian move expertly around the factory, taking what was right in front of their noses and using it to change the world, I felt a bit foolish. No matter how many trees I had climbed, how many tree poems I had read or re-read or written, I could not claim to have saved a single one. (The only one I'd ever planted was promptly weed-whacked into mulch!) I had done the little things—years of the vegetarianism, buying used clothes and furniture, voting every chance I got—but not once had it crossed my mind that maybe it wasn't even close to enough.

Now, here I was, about to go back to spending hours and hours writing papers about the philosophical implications of the Anthropocene—papers I knew Tom would read with a sneer—their contents hovering so far above the real, material world. And while I liked to think I could withstand Tom's teasing, I wasn't sure I wanted to. His criticism was a lens I could have chosen to side-step or dismiss as pesky, misinformed, and counterproductive, but I had come to like and respect him too much. And for all the ways he unsettled me, I was grateful that he cared enough to push me closer toward some sort of truth.

Outside my window now lay a dark infinity, the faintest of lights still visible from the towns so many miles below us. I felt an urge to get down there, down to Earth. I fell asleep with my head pressed against the circle of glass, the woman beside me softly snoring.

# Part Two

—

# Tom

## New York City, United States
### DECEMBER 2013

My first trip to America was in December 2013. I was eighteen, and I was excited—so much so that I couldn't find sleep the night before.

I was going to America. I was going to fly on a plane.

I repeatedly packed and unpacked the second-hand suitcase Baba and I bought for a mere 400 shillings at the expansive Garissa malls the day before. As I packed my black jacket, the one I'd picked up at the flea market in Gikomba, I wondered whether it would be enough for the biting cold of a New York winter. The trader had assured me it would. In retrospect, it had been foolish of me, someone who'd never experienced "New York cold," to believe the words of a Gikomba trader who hadn't either.

As it turned out, Jacob and Innovate Kenya had a benefactor of their own—the Rockefeller Foundation—and I had been invited to attend their "Next Century Innovators Awards." Innovate Kenya was to be recognized for their work in finding and supporting the next generation of do-good innovators.

Jacob picked me up at 5 a.m. for a long day of travel from Nairobi to New York. Our driver arranged my suitcase into the trunk beside Jacob's and seemed amused when my equally animated sister, Anita, hopped into the car for the ride from South C to the Jomo Kenyatta International Airport. We'd seen the airport, also known as JKIA, on TV broadcasts, but neither of us had been there in person.

JKIA was underwhelming. Was this the same airport where our world-champion Kenyan athletes were greeted by dancing supporters and government officials eager for a photo op? Even in the face of disappointment, we huddled together for a group photo, making sure the "Jomo Kenyatta International Airport" sign could be seen in the background. (That photo now hangs proudly in my grandmother's home.) With that, Jacob ushered me toward Departures. I imagine he didn't want us to miss our flight, but I blamed his hastiness on his whiteness. (Akweya, my high school physics teacher, had said that when the white man colonized Africa, he tried to rush the African everywhere, forgetting—to his eventual detriment—that *haraka haraka haina baraka*.)

Anita grabbed me right before I went inside and whispered as she hugged me, "Run, run away in America, Tom. Run, run far away. Far away where they cannot find you." I must have nodded that I would try, that I would try to run away in America. Maybe, just maybe, I would become rich and successful like all the Americans we saw on television. And maybe, with my newfound American riches, I would send Anita dollars, and she, too, armed with dollars, would come to America and run away.

———

If JKIA was a tiny fledgling, then New York's JFK would be the ogre of African folklore, a giant, imposing beast that appears welcoming but can be deadly. All the men and women in neat, navy-blue uniforms, with mean faces and cold stares, made me question whether I belonged in America's JFK. The customs officer's gaze was especially piercing. His eyes darted between Jacob and me, perhaps speculating about the remote African village from which I had been rescued. But my invitation letter from the

Rockefeller Foundation appeared to lift his suspicions. I nodded, half triumphantly. With my passport stamped, I was in America.

The Rockefeller Foundation put me up on the fortieth floor of the DoubleTree Hotel in Times Square. From my window, the city sprawled before me like a massive elephant asserting its dominance. Some buildings rose slender and tall—like elongated trunks—while others, relics of the past, were broad and short—like flapping ears. But up close, this dominance appeared a folly. The streets were filled with the chaotic choreography of pedestrians and vehicles, each fiercely claiming their right to space, and a persistent stench colored the crumbling infrastructure.

However, from the eighth floor of 509W 34th Street, where I first met the American "do-good" bourgeoisie, New York was a different beast. It was the rhino—majestic, revered, and highly sought after. The interior of the building conjured a radiant opulence that bounced off of the glass walls overlooking Hudson Yards. That morning, the bourgeoisie were in their element, with the men in expensive suits and the women in expensive pantsuits or flowy dresses, each sipping their morning coffee or tea.

Unless one is a part of the American do-good bourgeoisie, one cannot hang out in these spaces without feeling out of place. This was especially true for me that morning, wearing my ironed black trousers, white shirt, and black tie with yellow stripes. I did not feel out of place because of the strength of the black coffee, which, unlike our Kenyan coffee, was blacker, bitter, and unsweetened. I did not feel out of place because the waiters—dressed in white, with unfamiliar accents—carried plates of small bites that seemed weirder each time they were presented to me. I did not feel out of place because of the thirty-second conversations, the so-called "networking," in which one pretends to be intrigued by the other, only to dash off when they realize that person has nothing to offer. What made me feel out of place was the certainty, the conviction, the assuredness of the attendees.

Here, at this event celebrating the Rockefeller Foundation's Next Century Innovators Awardees, it seemed as if the solutions to the world's most intractable problems had been found. And they had been found by the American do-good bourgeoisie. I could feel their confidence, their arrogance, in the way they mingled loudly. I could see it in the glances they cast across the room and at each other. I could hear it in how the host, dressed in a sharp blue pantsuit, spoke powerfully and vividly about all the ways the Rockefeller Foundation was making the world a better place. And was she wrong? She couldn't be. She couldn't be wrong because this room held the donor class that wrote the checks that made the world a better place, the financiers that managed the assets that made the world a better place, the consultants that developed the frameworks that made the world a better place, the academics who wrote the research papers that made the world a better place, the nonprofit executives that ran the organizations that made the world a better place.

And there I was, an eighteen-year-old from a rural village in Africa, and I couldn't see anything to make me question that they were indeed making the world a better place. After all, had they not put me up in New York's DoubleTree at Times Square?

# Eve

## Cambridge, United States
### FEBRUARY 2019

I walked up the wide, wooden stairs of Harvard's off-campus Dudley Co-Op, then stood on the porch for a moment, breathing. I'd gotten back from Kenya only the week before, and the cold still took me by surprise when it made clouds of my breath. They dissolved slowly now in the faint glow of the porch light.

Above the door hung a sign that read "Center for High Energy Metaphysics." I knew just enough about both energy and metaphysics to feel this was either a wonderful joke or a prospective concept that I was genuinely excited about if real—I imagined a table of over-caffeinated philosophers. I later learned that some preferred the abbreviation "Center for HEMP." All of these interpretations felt inviting.

There was something about stepping just outside the orbit of campus and its unique, archaic laws of gravity that seemed to create some new forcefield, the laws of which were not yet clear. I raised my arm to knock.

I'd found my way there because of a poster. Earlier that day, as the February air hustled me to class, a neon orange paper on a bulletin board caught my eye. Something about the color and the words "ExxonMobil" and "the Harvard Corporation" made me stop short on the slushy walkway.

I took out my phone to jot down the contact email, my fingers stinging in the cold. Long black coats streamed past on either side of me. Life back in Cambridge did not spill slowly and brightly onto sidewalks like in Kenya. Instead, it shuffled efficiently around, bundled and moving from heated building to heated building according to the looming logic of iCal.

Now, here I was, shivering as Isa let me in. She had been the one to reply when I'd emailed about the next meeting. Standing in the doorway, we realized we knew each other: we'd once spent five days together at a silent meditation retreat sponsored by the college's wellness program. I loved that retreat. It was held at a big house in western Massachusetts. There was an intense intimacy in the way all fifty of us shared the space without speaking, sipped coffee without speaking, clinked our forks with-out speaking, and shoelessly padded around the home's thick, beautiful carpets. Given the mandatory silence, I couldn't say I knew much about Isa, but I was pretty sure I liked her. Inside the Co-Op's vestibule, we hugged.

We were there to discuss fossil fuels, specifically Harvard's divestment from them. Others were there already, and I joined them around the long wooden table where the Co-Op's residents ate their meals. I had never seen walls so rambunctiously collaged or witnessed the home-brewing of such vast quantities of kombucha. There were about fifteen of us in total. At quarter past the hour, we began introductions. I was Eve, this was my first meeting, and I was happy to be there, I explained. With the exception of Isa, I had never seen any of these people before; we didn't go to the same parties or have any of the same friends. Suddenly, I felt myself being sized up, as if they were gauging whether I could be trusted.

The truth was that I had gone there because of Tom. We hadn't seen each other since getting back to campus, but the impact of our time together had not yet worn off. There were two questions he had asked that had taken root inside me and bloomed with a painful clarity: What was I doing reading books about environmental justice all day if I wasn't going to do anything about it? And why was I flying to Kenya when there was so much work to be done right here at home? A few months ago, I might have walked by that orange poster without a second glance. My campus life felt full already, with my classes, my job as a writing tutor, and my friends. And though I'd gotten somewhat involved in various Democratic political groups my freshman year, the 2016 election had left me deeply disappointed by both parties. Plus, some of the students in those groups struck me as hungrier for power than for real change.

At the Co-Op that night, there was none of that. There was a lot to take in. *Divestment*, they explained, is the opposite of investment—it means taking money *out* of something. Harvard has a lot of money. Students pay tuition, but the school primarily runs off its endowment, a pot of more than $40 billion that Harvard doesn't spend but instead holds onto and invests. When that much money is invested, it generates hundreds of millions of dollars every year in returns, and that money is what is spent to cover annual expenses. Most big schools run this way, as do most foundations, religious organizations, wealthy families, and the pension funds that pay public employees after they retire.

So, the poster's "Harvard Corporation" claim was not hyperbolic rhetoric. Harvard is literally a corporation—the oldest in the Western hemisphere, by its own estimates. It blew my mind to think of my school in those terms. Even wilder, the very same institution that taught me about ExxonMobil's suppression of climate science owned (via stocks) a piece of that company. When ExxonMobil was doing well, Harvard was benefiting.

In part, the fossil fuel divestment campaign was about moving money and pressuring Harvard to redirect its investments away from the companies that drill for oil. But on another level, divestment as a whole is about moving people. Like any social movement, it's about raising awareness, changing the culture, and bringing lots of people together to hold the powerful to account.

I was absorbed by both the substance and style of what was said; there was a subversiveness, a jadedness, and, above all, a sense of urgency, righteousness, and scandal. It was nothing like the other political clubs I'd tried to join at Harvard, where a confident club president would get up in front of the group and share some meeting agenda, play-acting the stiff vocabulary of a business executive. There was no networking, no application process, no bubbliness or arrogance, or anything else that suggested this group accepted the way the world was working. People were there because they were angry and/or heartbroken. They were there because the traditional avenues of change-making felt inadequate or defective. There was also a shared heaviness. It was a heaviness I had felt for years and had not known what to do with. Tom had made me feel so silly, so passive for sitting on the sidelines when clubs like Consulting for Business and the Environment existed. But I felt immense relief as I sat there, listening to others explain why they had come. This was what I hadn't known I was looking for—a place where we could sit with the raw truth that things were gravely, gravely wrong in the world, and we didn't have to pretend to feel okay with it.

After introductions were over and background information was provided, the leaders raised the business at hand. An important event was coming up. It was a chance to really get the attention of the University's president, Lawrence Bacow, who, thus far, had not acknowledged the campaign. He'd be joining a panel on the purpose of higher education at Harvard's Institute of Politics, and the plan was to "disrupt" it. At first, I didn't know what that meant, but it soon became clear as we discussed logistics: At what moment would we all stand from our chairs? Would we chant? Did we have signs? Would there be arrests? Did we want there to be?

As quickly as it had arrived, the relief I'd felt evaporated. All of this was wildly unlike anything I had done before. I sat in my chair like a fly on the wall: rapt, not part of the proceedings but not *not* part of them. It was apparent that I was glimpsing something already in motion—something with a past, a history, a context I hadn't even begun to understand. I started to realize why trust was so important here. Unlike your average climate club, each new member was not just someone to sit next to at monthly meetings; they were someone to stand next to in the thick of whatever unfolded. I had questions, but I swallowed them. As the meeting ended, I said goodbye with a tentative conspiratorial solidarity.

I stayed up half that night reading. It was one thing to get on board with divestment theoretically and another to risk arrest for it. I figured I should first understand exactly what it meant. There was a lot on the internet about fossil fuel divestment—what it was, the ways people fought for it, the reasons it had and hadn't happened in various places and at various points in history. I learned that a combined several trillion dollars had already been divested, that it was a worldwide campaign whose founders included a Harvard alum named Bill McKibben, and that its strength was in its numbers. Harvard was a particularly significant target. With the largest endowment in the world and lots of financial and social capital, it would do and say a lot if Harvard joined in.

Our last president had put her foot down a few years prior, decisively claiming it was a no-go, but the campaign had been revived just a few months ago by a small group of committed freshmen. Years back, there were panels here and there, meetings, sit-ins, and arrests. Not much had come of it. There were critics who said it was a waste of energy, that Harvard wouldn't do it, that it was silly and symbolic, or that those efforts would be better spent on things like sustainability initiatives or electoral politics. Then, there was the argument that other institutions, those unconcerned about climate change, would just buy up the divested shares, making the oil companies even less likely to change. The counter-argument was that stigmatizing the industry—taking a shot at its political and cultural power—would hurt it in ways that were hard to quantify but easy to imagine: political pressure to cut their subsidies and trouble recruiting talented employees who didn't want the shame of complicity.

Before going to bed, I took a warm shower beneath the showerhead that I'd admittedly missed while using buckets in Tom's aunt's house in Kenya, feeling pampered and intrigued. I still wasn't sure where I stood in all this, and I wondered what Tom would make of it.

# Tom

## Cambridge, United States
### FEBRUARY

I had been texting with Eve since Nairobi. Part of me—the part that envisioned Eve as warm and kind, perpetually on the brink of her next adventure—wanted to stay in touch. I had painted this mental picture of her with her eyes, shadowy and sparkling, holding the mirth of a thousand untold stories. This part of me perhaps yearned for what Eve represented. Yet, another part of me—the part that had been persuaded by America that only birds of the same feather flock together—did not want to stay in touch.

Eve and I shared nothing beyond that one week in Kenya. She spent her days with her girlfriends in Cabot House or partying at the Spee Club, one of Harvard's many exclusive social clubs. While I was juggling a passion for English ("You already speak English, so why must you go to America to learn it?" my mom had asked) with a more practical Psychology degree, Eve seemed to have embraced the essence of a liberal arts education, keen on dissecting the minutiae of Enlightenment-era philosophers' theories.

"Meet me at the top of the spiral staircase," I texted Eve as I packed my books, ready for dinner.

Eve was wearing a casual black T-shirt beneath her winter jacket. She seemed excited to see me; a broad, genuine smile crinkled the corners of her eyes.

"What are you doing up there?" She asked, curious.

"I am writing a manifesto," I answered. I wasn't.

Eve laughed, seeming to have caught on to my playful banter.

I gave her a hug. I had missed her.

We left the library and found a seat toward the end of the Eliot House dining hall. The space is intentionally curated to encourage people to sit together and talk; chandeliers provide warm light, wooden tables are spread out invitingly, and the high ceilings give a sense of openness. It was one of my favorite spots on campus.

As we sat down to eat, I told Eve about my History of Psychiatry class and how I'd started to develop an interest in mental health. Just that winter, I'd assisted in a research study that had concluded that one in two Kenyan adolescents was depressed or anxious. With that knowledge, I'd been increasingly thinking that my post-college plans might involve working in mental health across Kenya. Eve, meanwhile, was planning to take a class on the Politics of Nature this semester. I was intrigued; even nature, it seemed, had become political.

"I went to this fascinating meeting the other day," she said. "Have you heard of the fossil fuel divestment campaign?"

"Oh no," I replied. "Are we losing you?"

"What?" Eve asked, seeming surprised.

I knew enough about the Divest campaign to know I didn't like it. I had come to understand that Harvard had a lot of students who wanted to do something *impactful*, something they believed could make the world a better place. I had also come to understand that America was ripe for that type of activism, especially on liberal campuses. It was 2019, Trump was president, and the world—at least from an American viewpoint—seemed like it was crumbling. There were threats to democratic processes and threats to the rights of women. Add in the climate crisis, which appeared more devastating by the day, and I could see why young students didn't want to just sit around and study about the world—they wanted to change it.

But Divest Harvard?

I first encountered the campaign at the Activities Fair my freshman year. I was eager and excited. After all, I'd been working in clean energy for the past three years. Here, I thought, were people who cared about the causes I cared about. I signed up for their email list and planned to attend some introductory meetings. But after a few emails and some background research, I concluded that though we shared a common goal—accelerating the clean energy transition—these were not my people. I was a doer, not an activist. I wasn't someone who had read a few articles, listened to a couple audiobooks, watched snippets of activist stories on Instagram, and concluded that I knew more about the climate problem and how to fix it than everyone else. I did not believe that groups like Divest Harvard would lead to the type of dialogue and consensus-building needed for the transition.

"Are you thinking of joining the divest movement?" I asked her, worried.

"I don't know yet," she replied. "I'm trying to figure out what it's all about."

"Damn, Eve, are we losing you to the alt-left?"

She chuckled. Maybe she thought I was trying to unsettle her like I did in Kenya. I was. But I also didn't think Eve would join. She was reasonable and fair-minded. I figured she would give it more thought and conclude, like I did, that it would be a waste of her time. There were far more impactful ways to get involved, like the Harvard Undergraduate Clean Energy Group, which at least did some consulting work for real-world cleantech companies actively working on the energy transition.

"Well, I don't know if 'alt-left' is the term I would use," she remarked. "It's really not that radical."

"I see," I responded. "Well, tell me how it goes."

"I've been really impressed by their levels of organization and general gusto," she explained. "They have this bunch of freshmen, actually, who I think kind of breathed new life into the campaign this year. They are pretty badass. It looks like they are not taking no for an answer."

Goodness, Eve was seriously considering joining Divest Harvard.

"But Eve, how is divestment going to help?" I asked. "Let's say Harvard divests. Someone will just swoop in and buy their shares."

"It's about the broader movement," she retorted. "There are trillions of dollars already divested around the world. The idea is that if Harvard does it, then more and more institutions will follow, and collectively, we can make a powerful statement and, at some point, even present a material, financial threat."

So, Eve had already learned the talking points: It's not just about the money; it's about the *statement*. It always seemed to be about the statement.

"Eve, the way money works in the economy is based on supply and demand. If Harvard pulls out its money but there is still demand for oil, someone else will invest in it."

"I am aware," Eve said, starting to sound irritated. "But the idea is that even if there is a 'responsible investor' like Harvard holding the shares, it's not like that has really been effective in the—"

"Would you rather have a responsible investor like Harvard holding the shares or some runaway capitalist with no social conscience?" Now I was the one sounding irritated.

"Well, as I was saying, it would be great if socially conscious shareholders could actually affect change, but they usually can't, so it's better to make a bold, public statement—to make it clear that this is not where the future of the energy industry needs to be going—rather than clinging onto this hope that after all these years, shareholder activism is suddenly going to work. And besides, the shareholders want to see these companies profit. They're not going to encourage them to abandon their entire business models, which is what we honestly need them to do."

You've got to hand it to Divest Harvard. With just one introductory meeting and a few emails, Eve was all in.

This was not how I imagined my first meal with Eve would go. A heaviness was beginning to grow at our table. I was starting to feel uncomfortable. Was I partially to blame? I had stirred the pot. The fact that Eve was defending the campaign, which she hadn't even joined yet, was telling. She was going to become an activist, a clean energy activist.

The previous week, in the same dining hall, I'd talked with some friends about the concept of white guilt. I didn't quite get it at first, but that made sense—I am a Black African man from Kenya. Now, speaking to Eve, I found myself revisiting that conversation.

It must not be easy to be a privileged white person in America. In a world where overcoming adversity against the odds is universally admired, there is nothing enviable about living with a silver spoon in one's mouth. Perhaps for Eve, a white woman from suburban New England who had college-educated parents and a safe upbringing and was attending an elite college, there was a feeling of un-deservedness. Maybe she needed to prove to the world that she was a fighter, that she, too, could achieve against the odds.

Perhaps that's where activism fills a gap for privileged white people on American college campuses. Why not? Imagine realizing that the world, designed for you to succeed, is also immoral and built on overlapping and compounding injustices: sexism, racism, classism, and now a rapidly changing climate that appears to threaten the whole planet (though disproportionately at first). I could see why Eve would want to join Divest Harvard. It made sense, especially after Kenya, where she'd seen young people fighting against sexual violence in Kisumu and seen the work Ian was doing in Awendo. Eve probably wanted to do something beyond just studying the world. She felt compelled to act.

Of course, activism worked for simple issues, like changing a single law. But shifting an entire industry in a new direction?

"ExxonMobil, like all companies, is in the business of making money," I said as I glared at Eve. "Right now, they are doing it through fossil fuels because that is what is most profitable. But if someone else comes up with a different, cleaner, and cheaper fuel, the fossil fuel companies will be obliged to sell the cleaner fuel, or they'll be outcompeted into obscurity."

"The thing you don't get, Tom, is that ExxonMobil has already done everything in its power to undermine the energy transition to renewables, like funding climate change denial and lobbying against climate policy, because they know this transition is not in their business interest. There's no reason to believe that they'll suddenly do something to accelerate that transition. It's directly at odds with their profitability. In fact, they're probably going to keep doing whatever is in their power to slow it."

*Dear God, they've got Eve Driver.*

"So, let's say that what you are saying is true. Do you think *you're* going to convince them otherwise, Eve?" I grinned.

"Not me, Tom. It's an international movement—"

"Oh, international? As in, a few Western countries?" How just like America to claim to be the world, like with baseball and its "World Series."

"Most of the big fossil fuel companies are based in the West, Tom, so that's why the movement is happening there, if that's what you mean."

"Why don't you join an organization that, instead of 'Divest Harvard,' is 'Invest Harvard' into, like, alternative energies?"

"That's part of the of the platform! It's 'Disclose, Divest, Reinvest.'"

"Ah, but why don't they say, 'Hi, we are from Disclose, Divest, Reinvest Harvard?"

"Is that the branding you'd recommend for us, Tom?" Eve chuckled. She'd said "us." "No, but seriously," she continued, "of course we want to see reinvestment in alternative energy sources; that would be awesome. But the movement, which was started by this guy Bill McKibben, who's this awesome journalist who teaches at Middlebury—"

"Oh God, nothing good has come out of Middlebury," I joked.

We both laughed.

"You're ridiculous." I could see she was trying to lighten the mood, to break the tension that had begun building. "Look, all I'm saying is that I'm impressed by the work they're doing; they're getting the conversation started. I don't see other students going around and starting all these efforts to accelerate the energy transition. And it's just one approach—it has to go hand in hand with other—"

"You know what, Eve," I interjected, "I actually tried to join the divest movement freshman year."

"Oh really?" She sounded surprised.

"Yeah, I signed up for the mailing list but quickly realized that it was not my thing. But they still send me emails."

I took out my phone and tried to find a Divest Harvard email.

"What was it about the mailing list that turned you off?"

"You must be aware, Eve Driver, that they do propose some rather radical approaches."

"I don't know what you saw, Tom, but the latest science says that we need to be pretty radical."

I filtered "Divest Harvard" in Gmail and showed Eve the screen to confirm that, in fact, I was up to date with Divest Harvard.

"Oh!" She lit up as we scrolled down the screen, "See that woman there? That's Chloe Maxmin! She co-founded the campaign here at Harvard and is now a state senator in Maine."

Eve was thrilled. Apparently, Chloe Maxmin was so inspired by Divest Harvard that she ran for the Maine Senate and passed Maine's version of the Green New Deal, all at the age of just twenty-five.

"But you Americans are really bad at protesting." I needed the conversation to end; we both did.

"What do you mean?" She asked, curious.

"You are like, 'What do we want?' 'Climate change!' 'When do we want it?' 'Now!' Ridiculous! Americans should take a benchmarking trip to Kenya or even South Africa. They will show you what a proper protest looks like."

Eve cracked up. "Tom, climate change is not what the protesters want. It's what we do *not* want."

"But you're like, 'What do we want? Now!'" I said, making dancing and protesting gestures, "and you just sing and sing and post videos on social media. But at the end of the day, Harvard is still deep into fossil fuels."

"Look, Tom, making a nuisance always seems futile until you do it long enough that people can't ignore you. And then that's when change happens."

# Eve

## Cambridge, United States
### FEBRUARY

By the time I emerged from Eliot House, it was dark. Only as the night's cold moved through my body did I realize I was revved up—like the world was moving, and I was moving with it, and we were picking up speed. As I walked quickly home, "movement" felt like the perfect word for this divestment thing, and I felt ready to be swept up in it.

Meeting up with Tom that night, I hadn't known what to expect. Now that we were back on campus, I wasn't entirely sure what it would look like to be friends with him. He was prone to trying to get a rise out of me, and not only was I fairly sure he would rub some of my friends the wrong way, I imagined he would also look down on them for their privileged complacency. Still, underneath all his obnoxious provocations, my gut told me that Tom was deeply sweet. He was also interesting, his every word so reliably intriguing and impossible to predict. There was an art to all of it.

Then, there was the question of divestment. Despite knowing Tom's politics, I truly had no idea where he would stand on the campaign. After our conversations on international development, I thought he'd probably agree that if I had no place trying to fix his country's problems, then a better place to start would be right here at home. But he'd come down on the movement with a vengeance that surprised me. As the conversation continued, his tone betrayed something deeper, more earnest—I wasn't sure what, but it was clear he'd heard about the campaign before, and that he opposed it with a passion so sharp it was almost soulful. For the life of me, I could not understand where it was coming from or if I should trust or defer to it.

I'd been just as surprised by my own self-assured defense. After researching the campaign, I'd been wary that I'd missed something—that there was some glaring counterargument to the whole divestment idea I hadn't considered, or maybe something had been omitted by the media my search engine had fed me. But after hearing Tom's doubts, I felt relieved. That was it? That was the counterargument? He hadn't even brought up *fiduciary responsibility*—the argument that investment managers must be guided solely by their duty to get the highest possible returns—or the question of politicizing the endowment—the concern that it wasn't the administration's place to take political stances through their investments. I'd come upon those arguments in my research and hadn't found them convincing. Divestment apparently could and had been done before at other universities without compromising returns, and Harvard's endowment had been "politicized" before anyway when Harvard divested from South African Apartheid and tobacco.

It bothered me that Tom wasn't with me on this. But what frustrated me more was the way he'd talked down to me about "the way money works," as if, because I was both young and a woman, I didn't belong in conversations about capital markets in the US or Kenya. I'd tried to laugh it off, but his tone struck a familiar chord. It followed a pattern I'd begun to see everywhere in the climate conversation: women and children are the victims, alarmed and emotional, and men are the "rational" problem-solvers, the ones with "practical" and "realistic" solutions.

As I made my way home, whatever ambivalence I initially felt settled into a measured conviction. Divest Harvard wasn't some kind of panacea, but it was certainly a good place to start.

That night, I texted Isa to ask about the next meeting. I also texted Tom an article about revoking the industry's "social license to operate." I'd forgotten that part. Had I mentioned all their government subsidies? I couldn't remember. His reply was two laughing emojis.

———

A week later, I was sitting on a wooden bench in the foyer of Emerson Hall—named for Ralph Waldo Emerson—catching up on text messages before my Politics of Nature class. I felt a particular attachment to the building both because it was home to the philosophy department and because I was distantly related to Emerson by marriage: he was my great-great-aunt's husband's grandfather or something. I'd been kind of obsessed with the guy since I was little. I had read all of his books and had his quotes all over my walls. My favorite was from his essay "Nature," which described becoming a "transparent eyeball"—sitting silently in the woods, dissolving, letting it sink in that nothing, in fact, revolves around us or our species.

A girl came and sat on the other end of the bench, but I didn't look up from my phone.

After a few moments, she scooted over a couple inches. "I'm sorry," she said. "But are you, Eve?"

I put my phone down and saw a small girl with dangly earrings and a gentle smile.

"I am!"

"I saw you at the last Divest meeting," she replied. "I'm Nuri. I'm also taking Politics of Nature."

Her confidence was quiet and disarming. She was a freshman, I learned, but the first I'd met who didn't defer to me in the sacred hierarchy of class year. She was from Bangladesh and, with the most honest, earnest eyes, told me about her uncertainty around what to study, who to room with, and how to approach the whole "Harvard thing."

"When you were a freshman, how did you make friends?" she asked five minutes in, giggling in a way that acknowledged her bluntness without apologizing for it. The question was striking because I remembered asking the same one—with the same frank curiosity—in my freshman year.

By the time class started, I'd told her about my roommates and my other classes and the weird date I'd gone on the week before. And she'd listened with this look that dissolved whatever distance usually hovers between strangers on benches outside classrooms.

As we sat beside each other in lecture, I glanced over at her, earnestly scribbling notes about settler colonialism, sensing that regardless of divestment's nitty-gritty pros and cons, at the very least, I'd find some kindred spirits.

# Tom

## Cambridge, United States
### FEBRUARY

Saturday nights transform Harvard's campus into a menu of options. There are those who choose to spend time in the libraries-turned-silent sanctuaries, those who linger in the dining halls where meals become endless conversations and debates, those who attend concerts and plays where classmates pour their souls into every note or line, or those who opt to stay in dorm rooms that echo with laughter as friends gather for a movie night or gaming session. And then, there are those who choose to party. They might be found in the common areas of dormitory suites—filled with wide-eyed and eager freshmen. Or they might be at the Spee Club, one of Harvard's exclusive final clubs (Harvard's take on fraternities), a members-only venue where an invitation is required to partake in the festivities.

On this particular Saturday night, I found myself at the Spee Club, in the pulsating heart of a 10,000 BC-themed party. The air was thick with the heat of densely packed bodies, sweating and dancing to music too loud for what technology would have allowed in 10,000 BC. Ian was wearing a white linen outfit that left one side of his chest boldly exposed. An attempt to emulate some prehistoric warrior, perhaps. Eve was similarly on-theme, adorned in a white costume and crowned with a halo of meticulously arranged leaves—drawing inspiration, it seemed, from her ancient namesake.

"Where's the forbidden fruit, Sister Eve?" I asked as she pushed her way through the crowd with an intoxicated chuckle.

"And you, my friend, seem to have missed the memo."

She was right. I was clad in my African-print khaki shirt and black jeans, a decidedly post-10,000 BC outfit.

As a member of the Spee Club, Eve had gotten Ian and me the coveted invitation. I didn't party much, and the running joke was that, at twenty-four, I was beginning to feel the vigor of youth slip away. But one cannot say no to a party so aptly themed.

"Remember Ashri?" Eve asked as she introduced me to the girl she'd been dancing with. Ashri, a Sri Lankan American with a big smile and a warm heart, was Eve's "boss" for their Kisumu project. Like Eve, Ashri had nailed the dress code.

"Really wonderful work that you're doing in Kenya, Ashri. Nice to see you again," I said, shaking her hand. America teaches you the art of small talk.

A contagious joy drew us into the music, and we each took turns showcasing our moves in the center of the small dance circle that had formed around us. Ashri was a talented dancer, moving with a captivating grace and rhythm, each twist and turn executed with precision. Meanwhile, Eve had a habit of jumping in place, her arms waving with endearing disco-ordination.

Eve and I hadn't had a proper conversation since dinner at Eliot House. We had hoped to catch up during the party, but it was nearly impossible—the energy was too intense. Too much jumping, too much laughing. This was not the place for a conversation, especially not a serious one.

I still didn't want her to become an activist, not because she couldn't be effective—she could—and not because Divest Harvard wasn't a commendable organization with passionate people who sincerely cared about climate change—it was. But to solve energy problems, we needed energy solutions, and, in my experience, activists—particularly college activists—were quite poor at coming up with solutions.

—

I first met Bren Smith, a climate entrepreneur and fisherman, in the spring of 2014 at Echoing Green's Finalist Weekend in New York. The event honored the aspiring social entrepreneurs shortlisted for the organization's prestigious two-year fellowship, which awarded fellows $80,000 and two years of entrepreneurial support. Bren and I hit it off, and he invited me to visit him in New Haven a few months later.

I was excited to see a real American fisherman, a *mzungu* fisherman, in his element. My ancestors, the Luo people, were fishermen as well. Growing up near Lake Victoria (or Nam Lolwe, as we called it until some British man "discovered" it and named it after his Queen), fishing is still the way of my community. However, rather than catching ocean fish like Bren, we fish *omena*, the tiny, inch-long fish also known as the Lake Victoria sardine; *ngege*, a perch ubiquitous throughout the River Nile; and *mbuta*, the tilapia that is the staple of Luo cuisine.

In the fall of 2014, I met up with Bren at New Haven's harbor. He wore an orange long-sleeved shirt, dark blue overalls, and a blue cap covering his thinning hair. His boat—maybe forty feet long—was the biggest fishing boat I'd ever been on.

Bren had become a fish farmer during what he called the "height of commercial fishing in the Northeast." After dropping out of school at fourteen, he'd spent years fishing for cod to satisfy the enormous appetite of the American fast-food industry. Then, like the biblical Saul, who had seen the great light of salvation on his way to Damascus, he'd had an epiphany. In a season of unemployment, he'd seen the bigger picture: fish farming was unsustainable.

It turns out that fish farms, including the one Bren had worked at for so long, were actually "concentrated animal feeding operations." These

CAFOs, within which an unnaturally high number of fish are concentrated in dense enclosures, foster the spread of disease and parasites that, in turn, necessitate heavy antibiotic use. This chemical deluge then leaches into the water and destroys local marine ecosystems, which, combined with excess nutrients from fish waste and uneaten feed, create dead zones void of oxygen, where few marine species can survive.

At first, Bren thought the answer lay in changing what people eat through activism or a behavior change campaign. The better approach, Bren soon discovered, was trying to grow what people eat in a manner that can sustain both consumer preference and ocean life.

Bren's idea was a "three-dimensional system of fishing"—a polyculture farming system in which seaweeds and shellfish are grown naturally within fish farms to sequester the carbon and assist in rebuilding the reef's ecosystem. The system was low-cost and left a small footprint, and if scaled, it could revitalize the oceans and seas. But the real magic of what Bren had done was that he had developed a *solution* and proved that it could work, thereby opening an avenue for restoring marine ecosystems around the world.

———

That Saturday night, under Spee Club's dim lights, which painted every face with some shade of joy, it was clear that Bren's story would have to wait a little longer. This was a moment suspended—one outside the relentless march of time. It was a time for living in the present, not debating the future we were all careening towards.

As the night matured and the crowd began to thin, the music's tempo softened. Laughter grew less frequent, the silhouettes of friends, new and old, began to blur, and the air seemed to cool as the rhythm of the night slowed to a contented heartbeat. With the final song playing out its last notes, we emerged into the brisk night air of Mt. Auburn Street. I couldn't see the stars that should have been above us, but I imagined they were unfazed by our revelries, twinkling somewhere in a silent testament to the constancy of the world beyond us. The night had ended, not with a dramatic conclusion but with the gentle lull of a tide retreating. The energy transition could wait for one more day.

# Eve

## Cambridge, United States
### MARCH

Nuri and I wound up in the same discussion section for Politics of Nature, which meant that once a week, we gathered with a few other students and one Teaching Fellow—a grad student named Rachel—in a small classroom to talk about the week's readings. Rachel wore bright scarves the size of blankets and told us stories from the years she'd spent in Jakarta studying ecologies of belonging accompanied by her saxophone-playing romantic partner.

Nuri and I loved Rachel. She taught us about humanity's mental, legal, and spiritual separation from nature. We talked about the early days of colonialism in the US and the hierarchy that emerged: the various Indigenous communities living in relative harmony with the rest of the ecosystem as white people imposed concepts of "primitivity" and "civilization" in their attempt to "level-up" at the expense of those communities and the natural world. It was painful to revisit this history—like cringing as the protagonist of a horror movie does the dumb thing you know they shouldn't do. We also talked about present-day *environmental racism*: where communities of color suffer from the worst air and water pollution, often because those in power put a factory or sewage plant there (or allowed infrastructure to fail) and these communities are not politically empowered to fight back.

After class, Nuri and I would walk back to the main part of campus with a girl who studied comparative literature, the three of us continuing the conversation. One day, Nuri told us about her grandmother in Bangladesh. It wasn't looking good, she said. The flooding was getting worse every year as sea levels rose, but her grandmother either refused to move or couldn't afford to; it wasn't clear which. The heaviness in Nuri's voice nearly knocked the wind out of me. She had this real old-soul way about her. I thought about Tom and his mother: about how Kenya was so far away, and yet my own country's corporations and consumers were making choices that affected people there. Here were real-world, far-reaching examples of environmental racism, highlighting Rachel's point that meaningful climate justice is global and recognizes that the world's largest contributors to climate change are the least vulnerable to its effects.

But while the three of us loved the class, others only took it to meet a requirement. They weren't sold. "It's too hand-wavy," my environmental engineering friend told me when she decided not to enroll. "It feels like a lot of claims made with confusing words and no data." That seemed to be the sentiment shared by many of the engineers, computer scientists, and economists new to the complex and interdisciplinary realm of liberal arts. I felt a pang of regret for Rachel whenever she tossed a juicy, ridiculously abstract question about ecological theory into the sparse, well-lit classroom, and the STEM students slumped back in their chairs, looking confused and dismissive.

At first, their reactions really bothered me. I saw these students as part of the problem—so far removed from their own relationships with the non-human world and unwilling to consider the thorny political dynamics of the very technologies they were learning to build, they refused to even talk about it.

But as the semester went on, I began to hear Tom's voice in my head. And I started to get it: for those who spent their days solving practical problems using quantifiable data or learning how to materialize companies or machines, I began to see how they might view our conversations as hovering in an intellectual ether, with little to no tangible bearing on the world outside the classroom.

I felt desperate for a way to bridge the acute sense of injustice and urgency to transform our species' relationship with the non-human world with the pragmatic "what can we do next" approach of those who were more tech- and business-minded. One of our readings suggested that the most important thing to do was appreciate our interconnectedness and feel grateful for all we have. I tried to do this. I jogged past a Shell gas station and reflected on Nuri's grandmother. I drank coffee and tried to envision the farmer of the beans. I stared at my pencil and tried to send grateful energy to the tree that had died in its honor, promising I would do my best to use it well. I felt enlightened, yet useless.

I felt *less* useless at the Divest meetings that Nuri and I began attending more regularly. The campaign, I learned, included a dozen or so gentle and interesting characters. There were poets, scientists, and aspiring lawyers. There were students from Norway, Oregon, and Florida and people who never showed up but posted funny pictures in the GroupMe. Together, we had potlucks, open mic nights, and weekend poster-making sessions in the art center. It was a side of Harvard I hadn't yet encountered: friendly but not extroverted; jovial but prone to deep, profound frustration; and ambitious but with an altruistic inclination.

Most other students I knew, including many of my friends, felt relatively benevolent toward things like Harvard, the Democratic Party, and capitalism. This was not the case in the Divest crowd. I'd spent plenty of time discussing the pathologies of capitalism in class, but I'd never met so many people who talked so concretely about combating it. And they were all so bright and reasonable that I felt late to the party—as though, for years, I'd just been failing to connect the dots. Then there were the movement's brilliant faculty members, hailing from a range of disciplines—from Philosophy to Earth Science to English—and lending some extra credibility.

The week after the first meeting I attended, there was another about farmland in Brazil that Harvard's endowment managers had purchased.

The problem was they bought it from a group whose rights to sell it were questionable. Naturally, this sparked outrage among the Indigenous communities who actually lived there, as they'd been neither consulted nor compensated for the sale. It was unclear whether or not the university would forcibly remove these native people to develop the land and get a return on their investment, but the Indigenous communities seemed certain they would. As I sat and listened in the high-ceilinged meeting room, it hit me: colonialism had never truly ended. The same patterns of extraction and abuse continue today but under corporate direction.

We also Skyped with a researcher in California who was with an organization called GRAIN, a small nonprofit that supports small farmers and social movements in their work toward community-controlled food systems. The researcher pleaded with us to do something. The fact that he was coming to us, the students, felt wild. As I looked around at our motley crew gathered on faded couches just before dinner hour, I tried to wrap my head around the warped power dynamic at play. I wasn't sure what was crazier: the fact that any of us were here at all, thinking we could take on Harvard and its financial investment choices, or that the rest of the student body was in the dining hall putting whipped cream on Harvard-branded waffles while our leadership colonized the Amazon. Similar antics were also happening in South Africa, Ukraine, New Zealand, and Australia. My head was spinning.

I left the session feeling like fossil fuels were just *part* of the problem and that so much of how we'd come to use and share the planet was backward. And what were we, as students, supposed to say—thanks for reaching out, but there's not much we can do? Objectively speaking, that simply wasn't true; we could spread the word, rile people up, call upon the student government, chain ourselves to the Harvard Management Company's front door until they promised to stop killing the rainforest. But the tricky part was, if we started down that road, there was really no end to it. If we stopped short—which, of course, we would have to if we didn't want to get expelled—we wouldn't be able to tell ourselves that we had done all we could.

The more involved I became with the divest movement, the more it frustrated me that Tom wasn't on board. This was stuff he knew and cared about—maybe more than anyone else in the campaign—and it weighed on me that he felt we were missing the point. But there was so much I felt like *he* still didn't get, like that a bunch of individual entrepreneurs starting new energy companies was not going to transform these global energy and resource extraction systems. They were just too big. We needed to band together. I wondered if maybe all of Tom's fundraising efforts had led him to feel a sense of competition between different approaches; after all, there are only so many spots in an Echoing Green Fellowship cohort. Still, I kept finding myself drawn back to Tom's mother crouched over the flaming charcoal, and a pit would take shape in my stomach—one that hadn't been there before.

———

To avoid fighting about climate change, we danced.

Tom and I realized we shared a love for boy bands, so we'd blast The Fray and One Direction and run around his dorm room belting the lyrics. And the way we'd sing—our voices so bad and so feverish; it wasn't just about the boy bands. It was about being weird without apologizing. Tom never seemed to care what others thought of him, which made him inconsiderate, authentic, or both. Either way, it was exhilarating: hurling our eight lanky limbs around to the beat of basic chord progressions, letting go of whatever socially acceptable radar had been buried deep in our mind's eyes to enforce obedience.

"#Decolonizethemind" was Tom's favorite catchphrase, inspired by his favorite writer Ngũgĩ wa Thiong'o. And that's what I felt we were doing those nights, reclaiming some sort of sovereignty and vetting our inhibitions to ensure we only obeyed the wise ones. It was an impossible task, but with Tom, it was always so much fun to try.

# Tom

## Cambridge, United States
### MARCH

There is a room in Eliot House known as the Record Room. At first glance, it resembles a typical dorm room. But within, rich hardwood floors are hidden beneath an ornate red carpet, and albums, ripe with the musty scent of history, are alphabetically ordered across two bookshelves. Two worn sofas complement the dark-wood aesthetic, strategically angled to face the room's centerpiece: the record player.

When we arrived at the Record Room that Saturday night, Eve placed her handbag on one of the threadbare sofas and walked over to the bookshelf. With the help of the small white paper labels affixed to the shelves, she thumbed through the records before picking out an album somewhere between "BACH" and "CHOPIN." I've never been a fan of classical music, but in such a sanctum, one does not admit to such gaps in taste. I walked over to Eve, preparing to feign expertise, but it turned out that neither of us was particularly keen on classical music.

We sat down on opposite sofas, neither one of us speaking. Our friendship had deepened as the weeks unfurled; we were gravitating toward each other with the gentle inevitability of falling leaves. Eve exuded an energy that was both captivating and envious. When we spent time together, it felt like I was caught in the current of a lively stream. Like a needle deftly jumping from track to track on vinyl without a hitch, her mind leapt between ideas, holding on to the essence of each. Her thoughts seemed to take divergent paths—each detour an exploration, and every return a deeper understanding. A bond was developing between us, but I couldn't tell why or what it all meant.

The record started playing, puncturing the almost sanctified silence in the Record Room. But we weren't there to worship at the altars of Bach or Chopin; we were there to tussle over the merits (or lack thereof) of the Divest Harvard movement.

———

Eve took out her phone and pressed record. She wanted to capture this conversation, and I obliged.

"So, have you become Greta?" I asked her. "Have you started screaming at everyone?"

"Well, I mean, the earth is overheating. I think it's pretty fair she's freaking out." Her voice was calm.

"Greta woke up one day and was like, 'I am dying from climate change, and it's your fault.'"

"We are all dying from climate change, Tom."

She had a point. But while we *are* all dying from climate change, some people are dying faster than others. And Greta isn't one of them.

"Do you know, Eve, that you are part of what many would consider a privileged movement?"

"In some ways, yes," she answered. "In general, activism and protest are things not everyone has the luxury of being safe and able to do. But if you do happen to be able, like a lot of people at Harvard are, then you might as well—"

"The problem, Eve, is that though activists have the best intentions, they sometimes hinder the very people who are earnestly attempting to address climate change."

That had always been my problem with climate activism in the West. It was too often the affluent, privileged, and white—those who had the least to lose—who possessed the loudest voices. After hundreds of years of Western industrialization, *now* the West wanted to address climate change and call themselves the "fixers?"

"And who might that be, Tom?"

"Definitely not the members of Divest Harvard," I replied with conviction. "The true experts aren't the ones yelling at the UN General Assembly or proclaiming that we're all going to die in 10 years!"

"Right, but the role of activists is to bring attention to those experts," Eve countered.

Eve didn't get it. She didn't understand. It was as if she was lost in a metaphorical fog, failing to see that activists—in their fervor to spotlight experts—were instead casting shadows. Our climate dialogue had been overtaken by debates on whether we would all be dead by 2030 or by 2050 rather than how to effectively capture and store carbon or reduce the cost of solar.

Activists seemed like one big lighthouse with a frenzied beam that disorients the very ships it aims to guide. They were crowding the airwaves, oversimplifying complex science, and dumbing down the discourse. When an activist cries, "We're dying in ten years," the average person wonders: Why bother switching to solar or overhauling my home heating system if we're doomed in a decade anyway?

"What ends up happening, Eve," I said, leaning in to capture the full weight of the room's tension in my gaze, "is that we lump entrepreneurs, scientists, and innovators together in one overstuffed basket with the activists. We politicize climate change and the energy transition, making it harder for the average person to engage with the issue in a non-political way."

"Tom," Eve interjected, "it wasn't *us* who politicized it. The fossil fuel companies and their hired denialists did. This shouldn't be a controversial issue."

She was right on that point. One of the culture shocks I experienced when I moved to America was encountering climate change denialism—an alien concept in Kenya and, for that matter, in many countries outside the West. Growing up, we all knew we had to do more to save the environment. We knew that green energy was better for us and for the world. The only question was how we would get from here to there.

"Well, Eve, I've only met climate science deniers and skeptics in America."

"Exactly," she replied sharply. "Because that's where the fossil fuel industry concentrated their PR efforts."

"But an excess of activism, particularly the kind that stokes fear, might be just as detrimental as outright climate denial."

"Without activism, all the scientific research won't amount to change. We need people to construct a political framework around it, or nothing happens."

"I can see you're determined to become an activist," I noted. "The activism I advocate for is the kind that funnels tax dollars to entrepreneurs and innovators. Imagine the clean technology we could develop if we redirected public funds to entrepreneurs like Elon Musk."

"Oh my god, Tom," Eve exclaimed, "Elon Musk already has more than enough money!"

We laughed. At least we still agreed on something.

"And even with all that money," Eve continued, "he hasn't figured it out. But these things are not mutually exclusive. We need both climate activism and innovation. People are not going to have climate change on their radars unless there are people making noise about it. It can't be this silent thing that is solved behind the closed doors of uber-wealthy tech giants. If we leave it to them, what happens if they either won't or can't find a solution?"

Perhaps she was right. Maybe we needed both. But not the kind of activism that Divest Harvard championed. Not the kind that declares we are all dead in ten years, anyway.

"No one is saying we'll all be dead in ten years, Tom. They're saying we must get to net zero carbon emissions by then or somewhere close to it. I mean, sure, fine, let's say they're wrong. But it's kind of like when you have a friend who's always late, so you tell them to arrive at 4:15 for a 4:30 event, and then the timing is perfect. If we say it's ten years, but it turns out to be twenty years, it'll be good that we said ten because then things will move faster. But if we shoot for twenty years and the better models were actually the ten-year ones, then *oops*, we're fucked."

"Eve," I said with a sigh, "that is very naïve of you, thinking things will move faster just because of American college campus activism and American timelines. Even if America—"

"Tom, this is not just an American thing; this is the UN."

"No one gives a fuck about the UN."

"The point is that the whole ten-year timeline is not an American invention, it's an international benchmark," she asserted.

Her statement hung in the air. What she, like many Americans, seemed unaware of was that these so-called "international benchmarks" often served as proxies through which the West projected its interests globally— veiled hands sculpting policies in distant lands.

"I don't think China and India are going to be abiding by this so-called 'international benchmark,' Eve."

"You are right, Tom, but that's why we have to be the leaders."

*Of course*. America must lead. It's their God-given mandate.

"And why America, Eve?"

"Because you are right—all these countries have to be involved in this energy transition for it to work—and that's why we have to start in America, which has been the major culprit historically in terms of emissions. That way, we can approach other countries from a less hypocritical perspective, to say—"

"What if I tell you that it is my turn to pollute; what will you do? I'm India, and I say it's my time to do what America has been doing for the past two hundred years—"

"Exactly, that's the challenge, but the point is that it's everybody's loss; it's India's loss, too, if they say that. In fact, many Indian communities are far more vulnerable to the effects of climate change than people in America. It's not like they can say, 'Oh, you guys in America can go suffer from climate change while we'll be chilling over here in India with a sweet, industrialized economy.' It's gonna be like, 'Oh, shit, now all of us are experiencing flooding, heat waves—"

"But you forget about human innovation and ingenuity," I added.

"I know it's going to be crucial, Tom. People are going to need to adapt. But not everybody is going to be able to do so, particularly those who can't afford to—"

"But that's the circle of life, right?"

We had reached a point where our dialogue seemed to chase its own tail. The room around us, with its walls of vinyl records, hummed with the soft melodies of a forgotten era. I wondered what conversations had been had in this room across the years. There must have been existential conversations about war and the threat of nuclear power. Debates on Vietnam and the role of student activism, on civil rights and if Malcolm X was too radical a leader. Vital conversations for each generation. And I imagined the music, just as it had been for us that night, forming the soundtrack for many a circular debate.

# Eve

## Cambridge, United States

MARCH

Here we were again. I couldn't remember whose idea it had been to meet, and I wasn't convinced the idea had been a good one. There was something about it, though. It all felt electrifying, and then exhausting, and then worth it again.

"But the thing is, Tom," I replied, "energy and enthusiasm for innovation don't always just arise organically." He seemed to think Silicon Valley had the whole situation handled. "The thing with the fossil fuel divestment movement is that it feeds upon a kind of anger, a sense of injustice, at all that the fossil fuel companies have done in terms of funding climate denial. And this pisses people off, and it pisses me off, and that's where the energy and enthusiasm come from. Political movements don't just happen; they are created. Movements have to hit chords. They have to get people—"

"When Henry Ford introduced the car," Tom interrupted, "the people who were in charge of cleaning horse shit off the streets of New York claimed that it was never going to work because they relied on the horse and carriage to—"

"You're right, and look, I think the spirit of technological innovation is great," I replied. "I'm just saying it's harder than it sounds to create a movement around it."

"And I'm saying I don't think we have to create a *movement* around it," he countered. "I'm saying that if there is good technology, and it's cheap, the average person—who already agrees that climate change is bad—will just switch."

"Right," I said, "So, of course a really speedy way to accelerate this transition would just be to make energy alternatives super cheap and super available. But how could it possibly be a bad thing to compound that incentive by also throwing a moral dimension into the mix? I think it's an undeniable dimension—this idea of there being an obligation to the next generations. If that moral imperative were to go hand in hand with the force of technological innovation, it would be a powerful set of dual incentives."

"But, see," Tom countered, "the problem with the morality thing is this: if I don't agree with Divest's tactics, then I am immoral in the eyes of the campaign's supporters—even though I *do* care about climate change, even though I *am* environmentally conscious. And I think this may be one of the reasons why, globally, the divest movement fails. Because by going the moral route, you're setting the movement up to be criticized as yet another example of the West telling the rest of the world what to do. And one could argue that every time the West has assumed a moral high ground, you guys have turned out to be completely immoral."

We both laughed, loosening up a bit at this flicker of agreement. He went on. "So, I'm saying, let's just look at this existential crisis like an opportunity for innovation and bring together human beings to innovate, whether or not they believe it's killing us in ten years, twenty years, or a hundred years, or it tugs at their heartstrings, or it saves them money."

I was starting to get where he was coming from, but I still didn't understand why he was so set on erasing the moral dimension of all this, as if "ethics" were a repulsive thing to prioritize. "So, you think innovation is a more uniting, galvanizing force than, say, the obligation to our children?" I asked. "Because our obligation to children is—yes, morality-based—but it's quite uniting, quite universal. For example, there's this awesome organization that we work with called Mothers Out Front, which is doing climate activism, and they all get involved from diverse political backgrounds but come together because they don't want to raise their children in a world that is doomed."

"I agree that the obligation to children is uniting, but I don't think it's uniting in the way the climate change movement thinks it is. Say, I'm at a Divest rally. It starts out with climate change, but it soon devolves into a laundry list—"

"Devolves?!"

"—into a laundry list of left-wing policies, so it becomes like *climate change justice* and *prison justice* and *racial justice* and *environmental racism*, and then it goes to *healthcare for all* and then *tear down the capitalist establishment*. So, if I came to the rally as a center-right person who agreed with the problem of climate change—"

I wanted to go into an explanation of how these systems are all inextricably linked: How European settler colonialism had ushered in the commodification of the natural world, extracting natural resources by enslaving and colonizing the people of the global South and exploiting their labor as they exploited their land. How industrialization—and, in turn, the form of globalized modern capitalism we know today—would never have been possible without the ongoing exploitation of largely racialized communities. But I didn't. I wasn't sure if any of that actually refuted Tom's point, which is that there are always going to be people who support the energy transition but aren't down for universal healthcare.

"Fine," I interjected, "so then you can go start your own club and say, 'Hey guys, we're fighting for a carbon tax; we're gonna go lobby at the state house, call representatives, use the Harvard network, do *x*, *y*, and *z*.' Do something different—don't just make fun of the divestment campaign and sit on your ass."

"I'm not sitting on my ass!"

"I'm not talking about you; I'm talking about the person in your hypothetical!"

We both laughed again, but this time, it didn't defuse much of anything. I kept my eyes on Tom's. He had started to get this look in his eyes that I knew too well by now, as though he wanted to seed my anger on purpose because he was afraid of earning it by accident. I felt my body bracing itself.

"Okay, but that hypothetical aside," Tom said. "Dude, I don't like climate change; I think it should stop. But I also want to continue living in a capitalist society, alright? And I think that, in the last few years, the conversation about climate change has accumulated like twenty other issues. Like my girlfriend was telling me that Black trans people are suffering from environmental racism, and I'm like, bro—"

"Tom, people have a word for you: *problematic*." I was close to done.

"But you get my point, right?"

"Yeah, it's called coalition-building, Tom, and it's important."

"If you really care about climate change, you should be building a coalition with the people who are fighting for carbon taxes, not—"

"Well, we need both! We need lots of coalitions."

"But right now, you are not building *any* coalitions." His voice sharpened. "You are antagonizing and alienating, as you have rightfully mentioned. Just a minute ago, you ordered my hypothetical person to go start a separate organization."

"I'm saying, in my dream world, people who feel like your hypothetical person should go and pass the carbon tax. Great. Then, some version of the Green New Deal passes. Great. Both things happen."

"I have a better idea," said Tom. "Let's find twenty Elon Musks and give them all the money they need to build alternatives to fossil fuels, and bingo. Because, if in ten years, we have cheap electric cars, fossil fuel companies will just naturally, without any legislation, have to adapt—for example, right now, car manufacturers are already moving toward hybrid and electric cars because they know that's where the market is going. But then with electricity—and I think electricity is a huge issue—if we imme-diately switch to nuclear—"

"I knew you were going to say that." He was on this little techno-opti-mism roll, and those always seemed to end the same way.

"If we just switched to nuclear—"

"France actually did some great stuff with nuclear," I said.

"You know what the Dean of Eliot House proposed?" He was grinning now. "That we switch to nuclear and then hire Elon Musk to ship all the nuclear waste to the moon."

"Imagine what the people from the 1960s would think if we did that," I said, laughing a bit at the absurdity. "They spent all that time protesting nuclear, and then fast forward sixty years, and the next generation of col-lege students wants to bring it back." Tom laughed. I breathed and softened as I watched him take a swig of his water—his drinks were always swigs.

"Look," I continued. "I actually think we need nuclear, but I'm wary of this mindset: that we'll just continue, or increase, our current rates of energy consumption by relying on nuclear. I think we also need to cut back our consumption, rethink the way we—"

"An increase is inevitable because of population growth. I know you don't want to get into the topic of population control..."

"You're right. I don't." I checked my phone. It was way past the time I'd told friends I would meet them at our favorite pub. "Thank you, Tom. I'm glad we...I enjoyed this," I said quietly.

We stood up and hugged. It lasted a few beats longer than I think either of us expected it to.

———

As I made my way out of Eliot House, I tried to figure out what had just happened. Somehow, after all this time, I still couldn't figure out whether Tom was the one missing the big picture or I was. Or, if somehow, both of us were. Before I'd met him or discovered the divestment campaign, climate change had never seemed to be a "debate" so much as a tug-of-war between truth and lies, powerless and powerful, good and, frankly, evil. Now, all that had exploded, blurred. I still didn't think Tom understood what the divestment movement was really all about—I guess I'd tried and failed to convey it in a way that resonated. But he'd at least convinced me of one thing: that between climate change deniers and divestment supporters was a vast and unmapped territory, and I needed to understand it better.

As I made my way through Harvard Square toward my favorite pub, I wondered whether some people are simply more inclined to tear down what already exists and shouldn't, while others are more excited about building what doesn't yet exist but should. If that was the case, then our disagreements had never been about carbon levels; they had always been more about our different skill sets—our distinct psychologies of hope, and the spaces in which we felt the most and least belonging.

But there was something else: how Tom bristled at certain moments, like when I sounded "too American" or particularly self-assured. It seemed like his objections came from somewhere deep and visceral; I could almost watch them rise from his torso, as if he were disagreeing with his entire body. This lent a kind of truth to his reactions, one different from the kind I was used to trusting. But it was *his* truth, and as much as it seemed to me to stand upon a slippery slope, I had too much respect for him to simply dismiss it.

Still, I was wary. I didn't like Tom's recurring urge to police my tone— sometimes I sounded too meek and humble, other times too abrasive and confident. Meanwhile, from the self-appointed moral high ground he seemed to feel he occupied, he was allowed to just shoot from the hip; the word "audacity" came to mind—though it was probably this same audacity that had enabled Tom to get up in front of investors at nineteen and pretend he knew what he was doing. I couldn't tell if this audacity bothered me because it was unfounded or because I needed more of it myself. After watching our last female presidential candidate struggle to strike a tone that didn't make people dismiss her, I still felt heartbroken and uncertain.

Tom seemed to set me off somehow, to force me to either match him or wilt. I was beginning to feel like maybe I didn't want to do either.

As I slid into the table where my friends had already gathered, the warm din of the pub and their laughter reminded me that friendship could also be easy.

# Part Three

___

# Eve

## Cambridge, United States

### APRIL

The amphitheater wasn't packed. Most audience members looked to be in their sixties and the kind of older person I aspired to be one day: attending public lectures, wearing colorfully patterned neck scarves, sitting elbow to elbow with her intellectually curious spouse. The topic of this particular panel had something to do with the purpose of higher education. As I watched people take their seats, tucking purses under folding chairs and slipping out of down jackets, the event, as a concept, warmed my heart.

But as I made my way to find a seat, I felt disoriented. I wasn't here for the same reasons as most of the audience. I was also running late. Scanning the crowd for familiar faces, I couldn't spot a single person I recognized until my eyes fell on a group of young people sitting in the front row. It was them I had come to meet.

But I froze as I considered joining them. I believed in this, didn't I? I'd believed in it from that first meeting just weeks ago when we'd developed the plan to "disrupt" this event. So, what was holding me back? I spotted a suited man striding toward the stage with a microphone and took it as an excuse to find a seat in the back of the hall. I slunk into the last row, feeling instant relief as I inhaled slow, deep breaths. The truth was, I still had no idea what to make of all this. Coming off my last conversation with Tom, I felt maybe the back row was the right place for me after all.

The fluorescent lights dimmed slightly as an administrator took the stage. As he introduced President Bacow and his fellow panelist, reminding us of the long, esteemed history of public dialogue in this particular hall, I was struck by the theatricality of it all: the hush that came over the crowd, the tension that hung in the air beneath the lofty ceiling. This space, called the John F. Kennedy Jr. Forum, took itself seriously; it believed, resolutely, in its own timeless nobility. Out of this stillness, the panel started.

It went on for less than a minute. The moment the mic was handed to the president, the students in the front row rose silently to their feet. All at once, the off-white banners emerged—glossy and angry. They flapped as they were unfurled from backpacks and oversized bike bags. Meanwhile, six students scrambled up onto the stage and sat cross-legged, facing the audience. I realized only then, reading the signs they held in front of their faces, that this was, in fact, a joint operation.

Having missed the previous Divest meeting, I was unaware we had joined forces with folks from the prison divestment campaign. It made sense. I knew that their campaign was also targeting the endowment's investments. The university was invested in private prisons—which, as with fossil fuels, was conducted through exchange-traded funds and with the same hypocrisy relative to the university's stated values. Later, our campaigns would spend more time discussing the ways these movements were intertwined at their roots. We would talk about the way prisoners were often sent to fight wildfires or held without air conditioning during heat waves, about climate refugees and the detention facilities at the border. We would also consider whether it was more strategic to join forces or remain separate. However, one of the things I would appreciate most was how we defined "solidarity." It was not about optics or strategy but rather the power of standing beside one another in the face of an intractable status quo. But at that moment in the amphitheater, it was all still new and swirling.

I couldn't take my eyes off the students who sat up there on the stage, silent and motionless. The chair of the panel scrambled to his feet and ducked offstage. The neck-scarved audience shifted uncomfortably. I wished I could see their faces and know what they were thinking. For some reason, that felt important, as though these ten elderly Cambridge couples were positioned to deliver a verdict on whether our point was well-taken. My heart began to beat faster. For another minute, everyone seemed to sit there with the same question lingering in the air—"What *now*?" I imagined this was not a question that arose often in this high-ceilinged hall. There was power simply in posing it.

Finally, the administrator came back on stage. *I come in peace* his expression seemed to say as his eyes darted across the stage and then the audience with all the grace of a floodlit raccoon. I almost found him endearing in his fluster.

His voice came out calm and even-keeled, but his tone seemed to betray a conscience almost as split as mine. "I understand that some of you want to make a point, and you can make that point, but I'm afraid what you can't do is hinder the ability of other people to listen to our speakers," he managed, striving to project benevolence.

But no one moved or spoke. I began to wonder: *did we have an exit strategy?* I remembered an initial conversation about the police at the first meeting but had no idea where the group had landed. The administrator reiterated his message. Nothing. Eventually, another suited man emerged from behind the stage and conferred with President Bacow, who rose slowly out of his chair. He had been awfully quiet up there; I had almost forgotten this whole "disruption" was explicitly engineered to ruffle his feathers. In this moment, he seemed almost peripheral, like the protruding tip of the iceberg of Institutional Inertia. But now, watching him, it was clear: He had feelings about this.

"First of all," the president began, visibly scowling, "I would like to tell you that Harvard has never had an experience, to my knowledge, in recent memory, where a speaker has been stopped from speaking. I hope this will not be the first time that that happens."

The silence was now ringing.

*Shit*, I said inaudibly. Not because he was right. His double qualifiers—"to my knowledge" and "in recent memory"—seemed to indicate he actually had no idea if or when this kind of "experience" had happened before but suspected it had, at some point. After all, this campaign was almost ten years old, and plenty of others had come before it.

But still, something had shifted in the room, and I was afraid it might be The Upper Hand. Suddenly, it was no longer just the problems of fossil fuels and private prisons hanging in the collective air but also this other thing entirely: the question of freedom of speech and the role of dialogue in democratic politics.

One of the signs held in front of the stage read "Larry 'Reason Not Demands' Bacow," referencing a previous statement the president made to activists where he said he "responds to reason, not demands." And sure enough, his next move was to remind everyone of this. He spoke with a righteousness, a total confidence that *he* was the one on the right side of history, speaking truth to the power that these students had, creatively, managed to assert.

"You can hold your signs in the back," he continued, "but we're all here to have a conversation about higher education. You're not being helpful to your cause, and I suspect you're also not gaining many friends or allies in the audience by virtue of the way in which you choose to express your point of view."

That was when he lost me. It was the first time in my life I'd had a front row seat to watch an ideal I held on a pedestal—the free exchange of ideas—weaponized against a movement for justice. How could he be so sure that in the face of these dual, nauseating injustices *we* were the ones off-base? Moreover, he wasn't simply sure our approach was wrong; he was visibly repulsed by it.

Just as my heart began to sink, the students started chanting.

*Hey, hey! Ho, ho! Private prisons got to go! Hey, hey! Ho, ho! Fossil fuels have got to go!*

In ferocious unison, the voices echoed through the Forum, getting louder and more rhythmic with every repetition. I was floored. Having never done this before, I'd forgotten chanting was an available response. It occurred to me that this, too, was a kind of dialogue—or at least an exchange—with each side rejecting the very premise of the other. Out of the corner of my eye, I noticed a campus police officer emerge from the balcony and lean against the railing. On stage, Bacow stood surveying the scene with unmistakable disgust. Had he appeared even the slightest bit conflicted or paid even the slightest respect to the urgency of these causes, I'm not sure I would have grown angry.

*Hey, hey! Ho, ho! Private prisons got to go! Hey, hey! Ho, ho! Fossil fuels have got to go!*

I began chanting quietly from the back row. I also took out my phone to get it on video in case it could be useful later. I frantically glanced back and forth between the police officer, the activists, the audience, and the president, trying to figure out how this would pan out. The balding, buttoned-down man to my left gave me a side-eye. I focused my eyes on the stage.

I felt a pang of shame for still lurking in the back row. But the truth was, I wasn't quite ready to get in the middle of all this yet. Ever since the run-up to the 2016 election, our country's political discourse had sucked. I did not want to be part of a campaign, however well-intentioned, that embraced vilifying the opponent and deploying theatrics instead of trying to understand those they disagreed with. I was still feeling out whether the Divest campaign was one of them.

This was why I loved my talks with Tom—they felt like a way to step outside the tired American scripts and feel the raw truths beneath ideas that seemed wrong on their face. But when I saw the president's face up there, saw his cold anger and sense of righteousness as he looked down at the students, I wondered why Tom couldn't understand that this wasn't about "reason" vs. "demands," "dialogue" vs. "shut-downs." It was about the inadequacy of our traditional avenues of making change and the friction, chaos, and myopia that occur when we are forced to move outside of them. But with a sinking feeling, I feared that he still wouldn't get it. I could already sense his disdain coming down on me, and in that moment, it hit me that the president's stance seemed to parallel the same patronizing tacks Tom had been using with me from the beginning.

I started chanting a little louder.

*Hey, hey! Ho, ho! Fossil fuels have got to go!*

As it turned out, despite what the chant requested, it was Bacow who went—he, the other panelist, and several audience members left. As they filed out through a door behind the stage, the chanting got louder. *Who shut it down? We shut it down! If we don't get it, shut it down.*

*Who shut it down? We shut it down! If we don't get it, shut it down.*

The chant continued. After a few minutes, the activists filed off the stage; only then could I see Isa among them. I got up to join her as the group marched out the door and into the street—the echo of our voices tightening then dissipating as we moved from the high-ceilinged Forum into the open Cambridge air. We continued chanting as we walked. The police stayed behind.

As the sun set later that day, I went for a run along the Charles River. I listened to my breath, my lungs drawing air in, off the pink water, and down, miraculously, into my bloodstream. My mind could only wander back to that moment in the amphitheater when everything seemed to hang there, waiting for some historical force to tell it where to land. I was still incensed by the president's callousness. I thought about the rule-following impulse I'd spent so much time obeying: the way the day's mayhem had grated so brazenly against it. I wondered if maybe that was a good—even a very good—thing for it to do. But I wasn't entirely sure. This was a "movement" after all—we were trying to *move* people, to *reach* them. We had to care about what we thought was right *and* about whether anyone believed us.

# Tom

## Cambridge, United States
### APRIL

If they didn't get what they wanted, they'd shut it down.

They said it, and they did it. And not even Harvard President Lawrence S. Bacow, one of the most powerful men in higher education, could stop them. *The Crimson's* headline was simple and to the point: "Divestment Protesters Interrupt Bacow Talk at Kennedy School." The cover photo captured the moment. There was President Bacow, in a black suit and bright yellow tie, with his eyes shut, his hands raised mid-gesture, and his lips pressed tightly together in a way that conveyed both resignation and palpable anger. Standing beside him was Dean Douglas Elmendorf of the Harvard Kennedy School, dressed in a classic navy blue suit and light-green striped tie. Unlike Bacow, he appeared to be keeping his composure, his attention diverted offstage, perhaps seeking a dignified exit from the tense scene. Yet the most striking detail in the photo was the protest sign being pushed by a protester directly in front of Bacow's face—in bold blue letters on plain white paper: "Larry 'Reasons Not Demands' Bacow."

The news article filled the screen of my 27-inch ASUS monitor. The headline may as well have read "WAR DECLARED." As I sat in my dorm room, the tension rising in my body began to mirror Bacow's—my clenched hands, the unconscious bobbing of my knee, the acceleration of my heart-beat. I empathized with the president. When did a call for reasoned dialogue become such an anathema?

I knew Eve was planning to participate in the "disruption." In the past few weeks, she had become quite an active member of the movement. For a moment, I let myself wonder what her role had been. Had she, too, held up a manila paper sign as she shouted, chanted, booed, and harassed? I struggled to paint this picture of Eve; she didn't strike me as someone who would do that. I had found her to be measured and reasonable. She was passionate but reserved and the furthest thing from zealous. But I'd learned that in the scorched-earth approach of American activism, even the most innocuous people can do very strange things—especially if one's goals are as "noble" as Divest Harvard's. The belief seemed to be that virtuous goals had to be achieved no matter what; the honorable ends justified the means.

I'd found this to be one of the biggest mistakes of modern-day activism. In adopting such an approach, they'd turn allies into non-allies. What had shouting in Bacow's face *really* done for the energy transition? How had the chaos, disruption, and mayhem supported the cause? President Bacow, by all accounts, was someone who cared very deeply about climate change. In fact, he seemed eager to position Harvard as an emergent leader in the energy transition—at least from his few public comments on this issue. Prior to taking the job at Harvard, he'd been a professor of environmental studies at MIT where he had, for most of his time there, advocated for a shift away from fossil fuels. But now, thanks to Divest Harvard's actions, he was branded an energy-transition pariah for merely calling for a more reasoned dialogue.

I had met a few activists during my GreenChar days—mostly young people under the umbrella of Human Rights Watch who argued that climate change was threatening the health and livelihood of Indigenous peoples in arid and semi-arid places in Kenya. But I'd found American activists to be very different, bolstered by a sense of self-righteousness and a certainty that stunts could lead to tangible long-term action. If I thought shouting and screaming were how we were going to save this planet, I'd sign up. But they had turned the conversation into political theater; climate justice was no longer the ceiling—it was the floor, and all of this was yet another example of liberal students on liberal campuses shutting down speech that they disagreed with in the name of social justice and equity.

Truthfully, I wasn't sure any of the Divest activists even cared to have a dialogue. It seemed like pushing the needle of progress was not their primary objective. What mattered was the publicity and self-promotion around it all. Not long after shutting down the panel, they were posting pictures of themselves holding their manila signs on Instagram and Snapchat; I figured it wouldn't be long before their friends were "liking" their stories and photos and filling their comment sections with clichés like "Go girl!" and "Speak truth to power!" But what did these hyper-privileged activists really know about speaking truth to power? Whose truth, and to what power exactly? Friday or Saturday evening would roll around, and they would fist-bump one another while drinking White Claws, proclaiming, "We did it; we shut it down. We shut down Larry 'Reasons Not Demands' Bacow."

Did they really think Larry 'Reasons Not Demands' Bacow had been so embarrassed, so intimidated, so moved by what he saw that he had gotten on the phone with The Harvard Corporation?

# Eve

## Cambridge, United States

### APRIL

The day after the big disruption, President Bacow published an op-ed in the school paper. The piece was called "What Kind of Community Do We Want to Be?" and the note it struck was one of lament: "It would be a shame if the state of our national public discourse, which has become so coarse, becomes the state of our campus discourse as well."

Tom texted me a link, saying, "Spot on by Larry."

I bristled.

The disruption fell a few days before a public forum on divestment that the campaign had been organizing in response to the president's push for dialogue. They had been intentional in inviting a student moderator from the Harvard Political Union, a group with the stated mission to "cultivate a culture of respectful, factual, and productive civic discourse on campus between people of all backgrounds and political persuasions." For weeks, campaign organizers wrote to the president to invite him, but his Chief of Staff confirmed he wouldn't attend. After his op-ed, however, this rejection felt increasingly untenable. There was speculation as to whether he might change his mind.

I texted Tom back, told him about the forum, and explained that it was time to see whether "Larry" was, in fact, open to having the very kind of dialogue he was calling for.

———

When I arrived at the lecture hall, it was mostly empty. Evidently, a Facebook event titled "Public Forum on Fossil Fuel Divestment" had not made it to the top of many students' Thursday night agendas. And the chatter I'd overheard among the student body that week hadn't exactly been encouraging.

"Did you hear about the Divest people who kicked Bacow off stage?"

"Yeah, seems like a great way to get him to *not* do what they want."

I soon realized the "reason not demands" line really resonated with some students. Waiting behind someone at the chocolate milk dispenser, I found myself privy to their take on the limits of free speech. "Where I draw the line..." commented another student to his roommate as he passed me carrying a freshly made waffle, seemingly headed in the general direction of libertarianism. Another student, waiting at the toaster, explained to their friend why prisons had been privatized in the first place. I supposed this was what the *zeitgeist* looked like in America as it simmered and transformed. It was a bit more bed-headed and blasé than the word's weighty German flare implied, but it was profound in its own way.

As we sat in the quiet lecture hall, much of the anticipatory buzz fizzled.

Then, suddenly: "He's coming," another organizer whispered from the row behind us.

"He's coming?!"

She nodded.

"He's coming!" I told my friend, who I'd dragged with me. "Bacow."

The truth was that even without the president, we had a great panel. Legendary professor and racial justice activist Cornel West sat alongside Jim Engell from the English department, Jim Anderson from the Atmospheric Chemistry department, and a woman I didn't recognize named Karen Shapiro, who turned out to be a financial advisor. They were all lined up in a row of chairs at the front of the room.

Sure enough, a few minutes later, the president walked through the door and made his way down the stairs. Without a word, someone went and grabbed a chair for him.

"Sorry I'm late," he said. "Let's get started."

Now *here* was something that might get people to attend the event. We seized our phones. "CORNEL WEST AND LARRY BACOW FACEOFF ON DIVESTMENT," we typed in our group messages. "SEVER HALL ROOM 103!"

As he sat down, the president gave Cornel West the chummiest of hand-shake-back-pats. "Here's how it's done, kids," he seemed to say. "Here's how *adults* do respectable politics." The back doors swung open, and heads turned as the trickle of students began to grow.

The discussion kicked off. One by one, each panelist established their profound concern over climate change as a pressing issue. There was passion and plenty of eloquence. But fifteen minutes in, I glanced over at the friends I'd lured. Their eyes looked glazed. I couldn't blame them; the revelation that the Bacow believed in climate change was not particularly riveting.

Halfway through the hour, the conversation finally turned to the specific question of divestment—and the president dove right in. Divestment campaigns, he argued, distract students from other important initiatives, like designing a more sustainable campus, and they push the burden entirely onto the administration. *Where was the personal responsibility?* he seemed to be arguing.

Cornel West responded with some beautiful words about the justice of *shared* responsibility and whipped out lines like: "You've got to be a thermostat rather than a thermometer. A thermostat shapes the climate of opinion by changing the temperature: a thermometer just reflects it." He also spoke to just how deeply indebted the climate justice movement is—in terms of language, methods, and ideology—to the movement for racial justice. He welcomed emotion into his voice as if to remind the president that it belonged there, implying that speaking about the nation's history of injustice and future of collapse with calm, cool "civility" was a whole lot easier when you have no skin in the game.

For her part, Karen Shapiro offered a lucid account of the limitations of shareholder activism, which I jotted down to use on Tom later. The president added that it would be more effective to engage *with* the fossil fuel industry, though it was unclear what he meant by "engage" other than perhaps wielding Harvard's power as a shareholder to pressure these companies to pivot to renewables. But Ms. Shapiro explained why that approach often fell flat; if the "ask" was for these companies to abandon their entire business model, likely at the expense of short-term profits, then not even the most impassioned shareholder could make much headway—and it would mean tough losses for the shareholder as well, as they would see the price of their own shares plummet.

President Bacow didn't react or respond to Ms. Shapiro's or Professor West's points. In fact, the whole panel was less a conversation and more a popcorn-style exposition of vaguely incompatible thoughts. I supposed the dialogue was more "civil" this way, but it also seemed to leave the audience with more questions than answers. Towards the end, Bacow just kept returning to the idea that divestment activists unfairly pushed the problem onto the administration, as if to say, "Building a more sustainable world is not our job; it's yours." That was where I knew Tom would have agreed with him most.

As I wrote down yet another note to discuss with Tom, I felt a sudden pang—the truth was, I craved Tom's thoughts on all of it. After all we'd discussed, it was painful to be here without him, and I felt alone in my dissatisfaction and questions. When I had told him the panel was happening, I'd done so more as a way of explaining that the campaign *was,* in fact, invested in open dialogue; I had not made it clear that I wanted him to come.

"How was it?" Tom texted me after.

"Disappointing," I replied. I told him that maybe the whole "panel" concept was ill-conceived—no way to let the spicy back-and-forths play out in a way that might get us all a bit closer to the truth. The Q&A portion had been a little better, particularly when members of the prison divestment campaign asked the president straight-up how investing in private prisons aligned with the University's values. But even then, his response was brief and unsatisfying.

When it was over, it seemed that no one but me was particularly surprised or disappointed by the panel's outcome. Most of the prison divestment advocates were unfazed, familiar with the classic tactic that distracted from the conversation at hand by centering the *way* activists pushed for change. Many of the other activists also seemed to have long since given up the hope that the University would ever have a productive conversation with its students in good faith. I was beginning to think they were right.

Still, I couldn't let it rest.

"What I saw last week was not a group of students looking to engage in conversation about things that matter to them," the president's op-ed had read. "It was, instead, an effort to obstruct the rights of others to speak and to listen."

Was it possible that we wanted the same thing?

———

President Bacow held office hours twice a semester. "Good luck," Isa had said when I told her I was going, drawing out the word "luck" with a tease. Very recently, the campaign had selected three members to attend office hours on its behalf. I figured it couldn't hurt to add another voice to the chorus. "You know we've done that many times before," Isa warned. "And I'm telling you, he's just gonna talk about the trays."

A week later, I arrived at the president's office. A line had begun forming from the door of the big stone building in the middle of campus out toward the grass. There were about eight of us.

This was the same spot Divest activists had staged a blockade years before to prevent the former president from entering her office. There had been an arrest right on these steps. In its seven-year history on this campus, the campaign had pursued all manner of strategies: a student government referendum, rallies, faculty town halls, and student meetings with the Harvard Corporation and the president. It was only after these channels had been exhausted that things escalated: the blockades, the arrest, a lawsuit. Then, eight Boston schools banded together and marched through the city, and the national movement grew and gained ground. Still, even as the whole social movement handbook was paged through, all that came of it was a very explicit rejection from the Harvard president, followed by a significant increase in oil and gas investments.

Eventually, an administrator opened the door and let us in. We each added our names to a list, signing up for time slots that afternoon. I wondered what the others in line were hoping to talk about—was I part of a little grievance parade, or was I among fans or even tourists?

When I returned for my 1:20–1:35 slot, I was handed a form. If I wanted to see the president, I'd have to sign a paper promising our chat was off the record.

I signed it. For that reason, I will only say one thing about it: I "had a seat" at that "table" in a way that made a mockery of the idiom.

Perhaps I should not have expected anything different: not after my long, winding, and unsuccessful attempts to persuade Tom, not after the other, older organizers had assured me time and again that this rhetoric around "civil dialogue" was just another way of saying "no" and "never." But I left feeling something other than devastated. Instead, I felt something almost like relief; I was free from some nagging conviction I'd been holding onto, some faith that there *had* to be another way. Now, I could finally concede: There was never going to be a real discussion. This was not a court of law or a democracy of ideas in which the most compelling argument won the day. This was a school. It was also a business. And no matter how well its classes laid bare the climate's dire condition, no matter how many of its students learned of the fossil fuel industry's skillful maneuvers to stall political action, its leaders had never been obliged to hear us out.

Isa had been right. As it turned out, as president of nearby Tufts University, Bacow supported a student group that pushed to get rid of trays in the dining halls. The initiative reduced food waste by 30 percent.

Trays: shiny, green, and good for deflection.

———

It had been over two weeks since Tom and I had hung out, and I wondered if he could tell I was avoiding him. I had so much on my mind that it sort of happened by accident. But it was also because I couldn't bear to hear him pile onto the whole "limits of free speech" thing—I hoped that the dust would settle on the campaign's recent disruption before we had to talk about it.

Still, when he texted me later that day, I felt a wave of excitement. We had so much to discuss. I couldn't wait to tell him about my conversation with the president; I knew he would get a kick out of it, and I desperately needed to laugh some of this off. I missed laughing with him. I wanted to just hang out and listen to music and talk about something ridiculous, like the concept of pets or the history of the Freemasons or whatever it was he was writing about in his alleged manifesto. As his name popped up on my screen, he returned to all of who he was to me: a lanky and curious oddball who, in the strangest ways, made me feel at home.

But I cringed when I unlocked my phone. The text had an attachment titled "Problematic.docx." *Oh boy*. This was a word that could launch Tom into a monologue about his hate for liberals.

"What is this?" I replied flatly before opening it.

A moment later, "Oops, wrong document." I had to laugh. Classic Tom. He sent another. "Demands failed.docx."

I sighed but clicked it. As soon as I read the first line, I closed it.

"What are you doing?" I texted back, my face hot.

"I am writing an op-ed for the paper about Divest Harvard," he said. After a pause, he added, "You guys are losing it."

Flustered, I opened it again. It was short. I read it in less than five minutes. Then I locked my phone and sat in my desk chair, reeling.

No good words came to mind to explain the betrayal I felt. But even worse was the shame. Not only had my efforts to bring Tom on board failed, they had backfired. I was sure he would never have considered publicly intervening in this whole debate had I not dragged him into it in the first place, and the last thing the campaign needed was a charismatic Kenyan clean energy entrepreneur coming out on the president's side. I kicked myself; in all my stubborn idealism, all I'd done for the movement was rile up one of its critics. Maybe Tom was right: not that *all* activism was counterproductive, but that *my own* bumbling efforts at it certainly were. One lesson of political organizing I'd recently learned was that it's more strategic to spend time mobilizing those who are already supportive of a cause than trying to persuade those who aren't. As I began to imagine all the new members I might have recruited had I not been so focused on Tom, I felt stupid.

I got into bed and tried to fall asleep. After lying awake for a while, staring angrily at the fake plant I'd hung above my bed, I replied. I asked him not to do anything with the op-ed until we could meet up and talk about it. I knew that he'd cornered me—that he would call this request itself a suppression of his free speech. But after a minute of typing, the three little dots dancing cheekily on my screen, he agreed.

In the dark, I thought back to Tom's snide grin as we sat in his aunt's living room, to how I sometimes felt that what irked him wasn't so much *what* I was doing—international development, divestment activism—as it was the permanent, fucked-up gulf between the opportunities we'd each been born with. That I meant well was something Tom didn't, or wouldn't, believe. No matter what I did or didn't do, it seemed he would never shake his distrust of privilege—that those with it could never truly be invested in justice. Perhaps it was why he always seemed to feel so justified in crushing my spirit and breaking my heart.

But what still did not make sense to me was that he found the Harvard Corporation such a compelling ally—or at least so much more than those resisting it, many of whom were students of color, many of us queer, a lot of us women. It also didn't make sense why he was so resistant to the notion that the entire climate problem was about power and its preservation. In fact, none of it made sense anymore. One moment Tom was disappointed in Harvard students' complacency, the next he was disappointed in their action. The only "action" he believed in seemed to take the form of charismatic founders with big ideas. It didn't add up.

I lay awake thinking about the ocean's waves lapping away our continents' edges while we sat on higher ground and bickered.

# Tom

## Cambridge, United States
### APRIL

It had been days since I last spoke with Eve. The silence hung in the air—perhaps a veil of avoidance or a shade of embarrassment over Divest Harvard's controversial disruption. Or maybe she was just caught up in the whirlwind of the aftermath. The shutdown of the education panel had become the talk of campus. Even President Bacow had weighed in via an editorial, something he rarely did. He argued that the protesters weren't really trying to start a conversation; they were simply shutting down other people's right to speak and be heard. This form of activist dialogue was, in reality, a monologue that reduced complicated, ethical questions to black-and-white issues. I agreed: climate change was real, and we've caused it. But the best way to stop it wasn't black or white. It seemed to me the Divest activists weren't focused on solutions because if they had been, they would have engaged with the multitude of participants, sectors, derivative markets, and so on that make the issue so complex. As much as we all hoped climate change had an easy solution, it was (and is) a big and complex problem. The matter required dialogue. The activists' focus, and by extension methods, was misplaced; and not a little reminiscent of a "white savior" complex.

What I had found to be consistently true, whether from my childhood in Kenya or my time at Harvard, was that meaningful, lasting change was gradual. And it was usually spurred—or at least supported—by innovation and entrepreneurship. It was at Innovate Kenya that we founded GreenChar. It was through entrepreneurship that we started a company that began the gradual shift from dirty fuels to cleaner energy in Kenyan households. But GreenChar was only tackling the first part of the biomass fuel issue: the fuel itself. For a true shift to cleaner energy, we needed to collaborate with those working on the second part: clean cookstoves.

That was where our partnership with Envirofit came in. Founded in 2003, it was the first clean cookstove company focused on the Global South. They created high-performance stoves that used less energy and emitted fewer particles. The problem was that their cookstoves were too expensive for the average Kenyan. In 2014, a competitor called Burn Manufacturing changed the game. To make their stoves affordable—and therefore more accessible—they moved their manufacturing to Africa, vertically integrated all aspects of their operations, and partnered with financial institutions (specifically micro-financial) to help families afford them. The result was a final price tag of $30 per stove and a collaboration with local banks that allowed people to purchase and pay off their stoves over time. Burn Manufacturing's successful entrance into the clean cookstove market pushed Envirofit to innovate further. Eventually, they, too, produced a $30 stove and established partnerships with finance companies to offer a comparable deal to customers. The result was a significant increase in Kenyan households' access to cleaner cookstoves.

The driving force behind this social progress? Market competition.

It's how my parents transitioned from using polluting, kerosene lamps to a d.light solar lighting system, which only cost them about ten cents a day to use. Home solar systems are crucial for the energy transition but often come with a hefty price tag. Many families simply can't afford to buy them. A competition-driven environment contributes to innovation—whether through new, more cost-effective manufacturing methods or collaborative financing solutions like pay-as-you-go models.

At GreenChar, we worked with an advisor. Kevin was a PhD candidate at MIT focused on decentralized biomass processing in remote areas and making biomass reactors more efficient and less costly. Because of GreenChar's entrepreneurial flexibility, we were able to adopt his novel biomass conversion reactor almost immediately. (Before that, we used a rudimentary reactor whose yield was only 10 percent.) Science is constantly evolving. As was the case with GreenChar, we must be open to learning and modifying. Our approach to the climate crisis can't just be reactive; it needs to be proactive.

Climate change and the energy transition are global challenges, and global challenges require solutions that can be applied and adapted globally. The Divest Harvard crowd didn't have a vision beyond the local, and that meant it wasn't scalable. Even if successful, the campaign didn't address the broader challenge of transitioning to sustainable energy sources. As a result, it—like so much of Western activism—was dominated by Western perspectives, which inadvertently sidelined the voices and concerns of most of the world. From the outset, it was the white American activist who set the tone and the agenda for what was worth fighting for. Conversely, innovation, at least as a philosophy, offers a more inclusive path to tackling climate change. It welcomes ideas and contributions from various global participants, all coming from different circumstances. For instance, it would have surprised me if the Divest people knew that some of the leading solar innovations have come from China and India, or that breakthroughs in clean cooking technology are continuously coming out of Kenya and other East African countries. It was my strong opinion that this diversity, in and of itself, created a rich pool of ideas and innovations that actually made a difference. At least, that's what I thought at the time.

———

In the silence, I found myself contemplating the role of choice and agency in the energy transition. As a youthful eighteen-year-old working with GreenChar, I saw myself and other Kenyans granted agency; we were not just bystanders, we had the power to make impactful decisions.

And wasn't GreenChar proof enough of that? Inspired by the success of Nobel Prize winner Wangari Maathai's anti-deforestation campaigns of the 1990s, Kenyan activists trained their eyes on charcoal. And they'd been relatively successful in shifting policy. They managed to get charcoal production for private and commercial use banned in 2012, and by 2017, charcoal use and trade were banned in Kenya altogether. Put simply, charcoal was illegal in Kenya. Yet, in 2019, the industry was still booming. It employed over 700,000 people and generated nearly half a billion dollars every year—the fourth largest revenue generator in Kenya—with 1.2 million households depending on it exclusively for fuel.

What Kenyan activism had failed to account for was, ironically, human agency. Alternative fuel sources cannot just be good for the environment, they must also be *affordable* and *accessible*. By contrast, an innovation-minded entrepreneur would begin by addressing these constraints, knowing the success of their products comes down to people "voting" with their pocketbooks. At the end of the day, if people can't afford it or access it, they won't make the change.

In September 2014, I traveled to San Francisco for the first time to attend the Social Capital Markets (SOCAP) conference, a kind of Mecca for those who care about the "three Ps:" people, planet, and profits. This time, my American benefactors put me up in the Green Tortoise Hostel, a far cry from the luxury of the DoubleTree. But I was close enough to Fort Mason Center, where attendees tackling the charcoal and cookstove problem had congregated under the banner of the Global Alliance for Clean Cookstoves. Now called the Clean Cooking Alliance, it brought together activists and policymakers but focused predominantly on innovators, entrepreneurs, and investors. The idea was that activism and policy could aid innovation and entrepreneurship but not replace it.

It was there that I first met Ruben Walker. He was a tall Dutch man who looked eerily similar to Jacob. He lived in Lesotho and had built a company called African Clean Energy there. They were working on a stove that could do it all: the ACE 1. It could be used to cook, provide light, and charge phones and could be paid for via a digital app. The company had already sold 10,000 units in Lesotho and was making inroads to expand across Southern Africa. Real, tangible change.

And then there was Ron Bills, the founder of Envirofit. He was an American man in his mid-fifties with grayish hair and a pale face that was beginning to wrinkle. I was inspired by how Envirofit had merged research and innovation with entrepreneurship to create efficient stoves that reached millions globally. They started out as a research group at the Engines and Energy Conversion Lab at Colorado State University—three professors working together to build a more efficient cooking stove that could save lives and protect our climate. And once they had prototypes, they convinced Shell to give them $25 million dollars to create a company that could sell them. Envirofit had sold millions of stoves worldwide. Real, tangible change.

Fast forward a few years (and even into the present), and a new company, PayGo Energy, is achieving more success in Kibera than we had at GreenChar. Their solution to cooking with dirty fuels was an LPG smart meter, a cylinder (almost like a propane tank) that provides clean-burning gas while monitoring usage and alerting customers when levels are low or when replacement cylinders are needed. Additionally, consumers don't have to pay for the cylinder upfront; they only pay for what they use, making the product more accessible. Today, some 10,000 homes in Kibera are using PayGo. Again, real, tangible change.

What Eve and her Divest Harvard friends were doing felt performative—like a mere pastiche of change. They were actors in a play, reciting powerful lines of urgent change, generating a spectacle, and dazzling the audience with the illusion of progress. But when all was said and done, and the audience dispersed, the reality would remain unchanged, and the gap left by Harvard's investment in the fossil fuel industry's ledger would simply be filled by another.

To make matters worse, I'd observed that in America, activism often added to the polarization of an issue, particularly surrounding the energy transition. In my three years at Harvard, I'd witnessed a kind of tribal warfare where agreement was rare and divisions ran deep. The market-driven solutions I was familiar with had the potential to cut through this tribalism and bring people together. After all, consumer demand often transcends political affiliations. And so, in the wake of the shouting match that had seen President Bacow shunned off stage, these reflections formed the basis of an op-ed I drafted for *The Crimson*. It was scathing. I knew Eve was not going to appreciate its directness, yet I believed it was crucial to bring diverse perspectives into the conversation.

# Eve

## Cambridge, United States
### APRIL

The only reason we were able to get into Annenberg, the massive Hog-warts-style dining hall where all the freshmen ate, was because the two activists I was with were first years. There was Claire (a classmate from Politics of Nature), equal parts fierce and adorable, and Ariel, similarly sweet and no-nonsense—someone whose requests I instinctively took as orders. We swiped in through the back door and hopped into an elevator. We were going up.

Overlooking the rows of long, wooden tables, at eye-level with the chandeliers, was a small balcony which most students never had reason to go up to. It was just after 6 p.m., prime dinner hour, and the sound of clinking plates, rowdy teammates, and awkward introductions started to reverberate and crescendo up into the high wooden ceiling. I had never felt closer to this special place. I missed it—it's where I had eaten hundreds of tater-tots and made many of my friends. I looked at Ariel, who was holding the rolled-up canvas.

"Ready?"

"Yeah."

I took one end, she took the other, and we leaned over the railing. As we unfurled the sweeping cloth, I realized I hadn't seen this one before; I studied it upside down. The thick strokes of blue and black paint formed an ocean wave, which curled into the words: "The waters are rising. So are we."

The hush started in the back of the hall, furthest away from us. Those right below us were the last to stop talking, the last to crane their necks up and squint to read the message we had silently thrust upon them. "Divest Harvard" was written on the other canvas in big, clear lettering—less artistic but more direct. Both were being passed around as part of a coordinated series of banner drops around campus. Claire held it with a quiet, matter-of-fact look. The silence hung for a second, then two. I looked at Ariel and saw her breathe deeply. I noticed I wasn't breathing much myself; the chandeliers in front of me started to look increasingly psychedelic.

And then, applause.

At that moment, I realized just what a beautiful noise clapping is—like rain after humidity. Cheering, too, which erupted from a cluster of particularly enthusiastic diners near the middle of the hall and radiated outwards. It was dizzying: the height, the echo, the possibility that all of this was working.

As I watched this shimmering applause, my perspective on the whole point of this movement started to crystallize. While many would never see it as anything more than an ill-informed mission to—counterproductively—move money around or a hollow effort to make change just by calling for it, this, right here, is what they were missing: the vast cultural and political ripple effects this movement had launched, that it had set out to launch from the very beginning. These ripples were sometimes hard to see, hard to measure. They resembled and sometimes merged with the ripples of other movements focused on gender, race, and sexuality. But as they spread, people around the world were exposed, one by one, to the idea that there was something deeply wrong with the status quo, including the continued expansion of the fossil fuel industry. And with that awareness, new possibilities emerged.

The impacts of the international divestment movement were already visible. By 2019, the global climate movement—of which divestment is only a prong—had inspired people on every continent. The ongoing movement took different shapes and forms in every town and region. Still, it was increasing the popularity of and paving the way for policies like carbon taxes and credits.

Meanwhile, the global fossil fuel industry was in a PR frenzy, as were many banks. Did the movements' critics think that all the institutions announcing plans to decarbonize were doing so because they wanted to? I'd learned that the term "carbon footprint" was coined years ago by the fossil fuel industry as a way of putting the burden of responsibility on individuals and consumers. Now, this movement was turning the spotlight back onto these companies, forcing them to prove they were not the villains of the climate story. And who did we have to thank for that shift? Could it be related to the massive rise of protests, school walkouts, documentaries, books, lawsuits, and growing demand for Environmental, Social, and Governance (ESG) considerations regarding financial and consumer products?

I had come to believe that social movements drive shifts in public perceptions, which, in turn, impact public policies and business strategies. It was difficult to point to. But if you took a step back, it felt so hard to miss.

———

The next night, I was back at the Co-op. Despite the thick wooden walls, I heard laughter coming from inside as I climbed up the porch steps. Inside, a small, chatting crowd had already assembled: more faces familiar now, some new, all red-cheeked and thawing. There was room on the floor, so I squeezed in behind Nuri, who was mid-conversation with a girl with curly brown hair. I immediately liked her based on her cargo pants. I squeezed Nuri's shoulder; she turned and broke into the biggest smile, glad I had finally come to one of the "bonding" events she had organized. She introduced me to the other girl, a member of another college divestment campaign at neighboring Brandeis.

"I like your cargo pants," I said.

After someone asked for silence, a guy with a blond ponytail and wide-set blue eyes stood up and introduced himself. He was another Brandeis organizer, but he was also involved with the Sunrise Movement. Looking around gratefully, he expressed how excited he was to be in a room of smiling, kindred spirits. It wasn't until then that I realized how much I was, too. This guy spoke like someone who had spent a lot of time alone reflecting in a forest somewhere; his voice was slow and ethereal, and I wanted to upload it to my meditation app so I could have it speak back to me.

In his hands was a guitar, which I had only been vaguely aware of until he strummed it—the whole space filling with a warm G-chord. He had written a few songs about climate change and asked if we would like to hear them. As he began to sing, his voice filled the room so beautifully that I wondered whether the layered newspaper clippings and colored-sharpie musings covering every inch of the walls somehow improved the acoustics.

Others then got up and shared poems. As I considered sharing one of mine, Nuri hopped up out of her cross-legged seat and softly announced that she'd like to share one of her pieces. As I watched little bumps form on my forearms, I wondered what it would take for me to be more like her—this unassuming yet fearless girl.

Sitting on that floor, I'd never felt less alone in my grief or more aware that it was so widely shared—that young people all around the world were also grieving and gathering to pay tribute with songs and poems and living in ways that honored all that's been lost: the traditions, the species, the ways of seeing and knowing and being together. This movement was *deep*. I felt it in places within myself that I'd forgotten were there. I wasn't even sure that my body was even holding all that I *was* in that moment; so thin had the membranes grown between everyone in that space—all of us just creatures made of carbon, that terrifying molecule of life.

We all walked back to campus together, the night feeling vast, as it should. I could see us, a train of twenty 20-somethings, crawling across the Earth, barely noticeable from the top of a tall building, invisible from a plane, insignificant from the distance at which the great Earthrise photo was snapped. It was stunning, the scale—and the fact that so many young people had become mobilized around the thin layer of atmosphere encasing our round and spinning rock. There we all were, trying to transcend something about our human limits, to somehow weave multinational C-suites, our college president, and farmers in Kenya and Brazil and California into a single, scary story. And in the same breath, trying to be humbler: to remind ourselves and each other that we are nothing without the water, air, and soil around us.

Nuri and I were feeling goofy as we walked. The air was just beginning to betray the whisper of springtime. It was the kind of night that bulbs must be evolved to detect, to take as an invitation, and we didn't even ruin it by wondering if it was coming too early this year—as if casting dystopia over warm weather was going to do anything to cool it down. We skipped through the yard, lifting our knees high just to savor the absurdity for a moment.

I hated Tom for denying me this feeling for so many months, for insisting that whatever holy unity this movement promised was false, naïve, and short-sighted. If only he could let himself be enveloped, carried away—I knew he, too, would have fallen in love with it. And it struck me how desperately I wanted this for him. I wanted him to look around and feel that he belonged here, to know that he did not have to bear the weight of the warming world alone.

Nuri and I sang as we walked. Tom loved to sing; he and I loved to sing badly together. After everything, I still missed him. I missed the way he abandoned himself to each moment, just as I was doing tonight—the way he would rather feel everything, the lows as much as the highs, than live as anyone other than exactly who he was. I wanted him next to me, sharing in this moment, telling me that at the end of the day, we were on the same team.

But that was just it: I knew as we said our goodbyes in the dark, that this was not a crowd in which Tom would ever feel at home. The careful choices of words, the disdain for capitalism, the way holding up a banner earned the status of "action"—and then, of course, the crunchiness, the femininity.

As I hugged Nuri goodbye, I was hit with the sinking feeling that these could never be Tom's people, not in the way they could be mine. And no matter how many times or how many ways I hurled divestment talking points at him, I was never going to change that.

---

# Tom

## Cambridge, United States

### APRIL

It was Sunday afternoon. Winter had given way to spring, and the air was alive with anticipation for Yard Fest, Harvard Yard's sprawling outdoor concert. In the Eliot House courtyard, the once-bare green space had transformed into a lively patchwork of picnic blankets, with people playing Frisbee and spikeball, drinking Bud Light and taking vodka shots, and practicing their dance moves to Loud Luxury's "Body."

Eve and I had agreed to meet there to discuss my op-ed before its publication. I knew she was livid, and I, too, had transferred my frustration and anger at the movement's actions squarely upon her shoulders. Now, we walked silently into the empty dining hall, made possible by the day's variety of outdoor dining options.

"No Yard Fest for you?" Eve asked, her green floral blouse and black jeans a stark contrast to the solitude of the room. Her face was flushed, as if she'd dipped into the Yard's festivities.

"I'm practicing a bit of civil disobedience," I replied with a smile.

Eve sighed, visibly exasperated. "Tom, I've little patience left for this."

We were both on edge, each trying to keep our emotions in check, knowing full well that letting them loose could unleash chaos.

"But isn't it your Divest Harvard antics that are up for debate?" I volleyed, unable to resist.

"Why are you being so confrontational?"

"Am I? I'm just concerned about the precedent set by disruptive events like these."

Eve leaned forward earnestly. "But Tom, they still had their talk. They just moved it to another room after the disruption. And shouldn't people concerned about the role of higher education understand our cause?"

"I doubt they left feeling sympathetic."

"And you know this how? Did you speak with them?"

"Did you?" I parried, the standoff growing more pronounced. It seemed as if we were about to spiral, each of us entrenching deeper into our positions.

"The point is, Tom, that one act of disruption—which barely nudged the event off its course—was a necessary evil. It's been four years of being ignored, of peaceful, civil attempts at engagement being brushed aside." Eve sighed. I could sense the frustration in her voice.

"Where is the clarity if you are just yelling and chanting? How do you start any meaningful dialogue with demands?"

"It's rhetoric, Tom. Rhetoric crystallizes our goals, moves us from vague grievances to clear, actionable requests."

"Last I checked, yelling and chanting are not considered cutting-edge rhetoric."

"Yelling and chanting are *always* part of social movements—not just on college campuses but around the world, in streets, in front of capitals, in marches and protests. It happens when all the other channels of change have failed. It's not the first approach. If people hadn't been aware of climate change and complacent in addressing it for four decades, we wouldn't be at this point."

"So, you're saying decades of climate awareness have led to nothing? That we're all suddenly enlightened by campus protests?" I asked, unable to hide my cynicism.

Eve's frustration peaked. "It's not about a sudden awakening, Tom. It's about recognizing that we're out of time for half-measures. Radical action is the only way forward."

It seemed as if the air between us crackled with the tension that precedes a storm. Words—sharp and laden with emotions—bounced off the walls of the chasm that had formed between us.

What would Divest Harvard really achieve? What if some hedge fund in Saudi Arabia picked up the University's fossil fuel tab? Plus, did the campaign actually think that Harvard's divestment would accelerate the energy transition as a whole? Would the $500 billion from university endowments in the US alone just disappear because Harvard had shown "leadership?"

"Come on, Eve, this is plain and simple virtue signaling. Nothing else," I said, my voice raised now more than before. "Unfortunately, virtues don't rule the world, interests do."

Eve's cheeks were flushed, her breaths coming in quick succession, mirroring my own racing heart. An anger had been simmering just beneath the surface of our dialogue for some time. This wasn't a conversation. This wasn't an attempt at common ground. This was a clash of ideas and ideals. I looked into Eve's eyes, and I saw that she knew and felt what I felt: that in this moment, our friendship was being tested in the fire of our passions and our wounded egos, and with each exchange, each continued stoking, the outcome was certain—a friendship burned, the damage potentially irreparable.

"I think you want to write this op-ed, Tom, because you want to make this argument about liberal intolerance. You are being petty. You are not seeing the big picture of climate change. You are not seeing this powerful grassroots movement that is coming together to accelerate the energy transition. You don't get it, Tom."

"*Oh my god!* The world's richest divestment movement is now a *grassroots* movement?" I interjected. Oh, the irony.

"It *is* a grassroots movement. It was started by Bill McKibben and 350.org, and it's growing on university campuses around the world. And it's grassroots in the sense that it's opposing powerful corporate interests."

Eve's disappointment sliced through the heated cafeteria air. The tension wrapped around us like a thick vine, choking the remnants of our friendship. Our once solid foundation—built on mutual respect and shared dreams—now teetered on the brink of collapse, threatened by the very convictions that had drawn us together.

"It's attitudes like yours—assuming a few experts can solve everything—that are holding us back," Eve said.

I took a deep breath. "But your movement is misguided," I countered. "Your understanding of divestment and your tactics are extreme."

"Every social movement faced opposition to its tactics. Change requires disruption."

I stared at her without saying anything.

"I'm still going to submit the op-ed, Eve," I stated firmly.

"By submitting it, you will be joining Bacow in framing this campaign as some naïve and intolerant liberal fairytale when you know that the climate justice movement is about so much more than that. And if it's worth it for you—to feel that sweet satisfaction of standing on your moral high ground, with no skin in the game—if it's more important to you than finding a way to facilitate the energy transition, then that's your decision to make. But I've got to go now. Goodbye."

She did not wave goodbye. She did not make eye contact. She simply stood up and left.

# Eve

## Cambridge, United States
### APRIL

It was bitterly cold and rainy—not the kind of conditions that would have invited hordes of students to wander over to Tercentenary Theater to check out what the commotion was all about. Admittedly, it was ironic (and somewhat humbling) that our rally was undermined by unseasonable chilliness, but this was Boston's April, full of false promises. We would have to earn each member of our crowd—every last one.

It was the final day of "Heat Week"—a double entendre invoking both planetary warming and the campaign's mounting pressure on the university—and the past few afternoons had been filled with panels and press conferences. The still-small, still-committed group of mostly freshmen had worked long hours recruiting speakers, booking rooms, pubbing events, handling tech support—the teamwork was spectacular. Before the rally, I went to the library and printed out a hundred copies of a fact sheet I'd made explaining "divestment" and why we were advocating for it. As I walked to the dining hall to pass them out, it began to rain harder: sharp, mean rain, the kind that leaves your knuckles raw and your flyers soggy.

That morning, I came across a picture from April 24, 1978. It was an epic shot of 1,500 protestors (the crowd was so big it filled Tercentenary

Theater) all gathered to call for divestment from Apartheid South Africa. On the stairs, several leaders held hands, raising them into the air. Out in the crowd, more arms were raised as people cheered in unison. There were protestors up on the platforms framing Widener Library, some holding massive signs and banners. Even in black and white, I could feel the collective effervescence—a faint sense of the chills I might have felt had I been there. In the background, I recognized the trees that still stood on campus, making it feel like a tidy, scattered forest. Forty-one years and two days later, I was worried. *1500 people? Could we get 1500 people to come get cold and wet and angry about fossil fuels?* The whole day, I found myself fixated on that number, convinced that if only our turnout was big enough, we might finally be considered a force to be reckoned with.

I arrived early in my neon orange Divest T-shirt to help set up. The amplifier shrieked when we plugged it in, and a few people hustling by on their way to indoor heating turned their heads. We must have looked intrepid up there, or insane—and I was very on board with it. Despite the blustery conditions, more and more orange shirts began assembling, along with orange headbands and hair scrunchies, a faded pair of orange leggings, and orange pigtails. We grew warm with adrenaline and camaraderie. Morale was high.

As my friends began arriving in spirited pairs and groups, I relaxed; I shouldn't have doubted them but realized that I had. That I'd been steeling myself for a series of texts and flaky excuses saying that, in the end, they wouldn't be able to make it. But no—even my French Social Thought classmates I'd invited that morning came! They looked so cute and committed, all huddled together under umbrellas. I passed out orange stickers.

I didn't invite Tom. He would have seen my social media posts, but I knew he wouldn't come. I tried to push him out of my mind. I'd never lost a friend over politics. But that day, I felt lightened by the possibility that I would never speak with him again. He had been tugging at me from my center in a way that threatened to unravel me altogether. I felt it in my body, this cruel urge to snip him off my sleeve like a loose string on a sweater.

At 3:30, we kicked things off. There was quite a lineup. The Mayor of Cambridge spoke, followed by a representative of the prison divestment campaign and a mother-and-son duo from Mothers Out Front. Finally, our star, Jamie Margolin, took the stage. Seventeen and ferocious, she was a leader of the national youth climate movement, and she grabbed the mic with the conviction of a veteran rally-er.

"They're educating us for a future that will not even exist!" she cried, the amplifier blasting her blinding moral certainty across the sea of umbrellas. "We have to WAKE UP!" As she continued, I found myself wincing a bit from the *eeee* of the sound system as it struggled to adjust from the amplitude of the mayor and mother to that of Gen Z.

As with the public forum, the group in attendance was a combination of students and nonstudents: there were a lot of crunchy-looking characters of various ages whom I assumed to be Cambridge residents. Many were over sixty. I supposed since it was a Friday afternoon, most people were probably at work. I knew Tom would have found the demographics funny. Through the rain, I could almost hear him cracking a joke about how much time we all must have on our hands to be out here chanting, jumping, and sign-making. I could also hear him saying, "You can stand out there all you want, but nobody with the power to do anything is listening."

It had been weeks since we'd last spoken: how had his taunting still not left me?

At the end of the event, a local marching band began playing to wrap things up. They wore red rain gear, which was good because it was really coming down now. My toes and fingers were numb, and I cinched my raincoat's hood around my face like a nut. In a line circling the stage, the band played—undaunted, displaying impressive circulation in their extremities.

Suddenly, a flash of neon orange flew up onto the stage. It was a girl from the campaign, and she started dancing. Others ran to join her. The band played louder. As it did, the prospect of flailing gleefully in the rain unplugged the sound of Tom from inside my head. I ran up to join the party. As the sound of drums and trumpets and a freestyling trombone lured more people up, I thought, *There is power here*. I could feel it. This was a thing with legs and stamina: a community of voices that would keep talking, that would only get older and louder. Our crew, romping in the rain, was small but devoted, and if nothing else, we could take pride in having made something out of nothing, sound out of silence. It was beautiful, the way everyone danced—subversive and defiant of the odds stacked against us. The people who had left, who had never come, who had laughed at us: they were the ones who were afraid, who were doing the easier thing. And we could challenge them by saying, "Well, what's *your* big idea?" And even if that was all this moment was, it was enormous.

When the music ended, the cold scattered everyone quickly. The dancing had been the only thing keeping our blood flowing, and now a ruthless chill set in. Looking around, I noticed, for the first time, just how shy of 1500 our numbers had been: we were *maybe* 200. I tried to tell myself that was fine as I boarded the campus shuttle back to my dorm, but the fluorescent lights and silence were like another slap; it took so much work to conjure the kind of energy we had that day, yet it fizzled out so *fast*.

I was raw and tired and hungry. As I walked down the shuttle aisle, I spotted a friend and sat beside him. He could tell I was spent and asked me what I'd been up to. "Are we fucked?" he replied, laughing when I told him about the rally. He meant about climate change in general. "We kind of are," I said, not ready to kill the banter but not loving the tone of it. "I don't know," he teased. "Mankiw says we're fine."

He was kidding, but as I trudged up the four flights of stairs to my room, scarfing Chex from a dining hall takeaway cup, the words echoed ominously in my mind like an overwrought horror movie. *Mankiw says we're fine*. Dr. Greg Mankiw was (and still is) an economics professor at Harvard. He teaches introductory economics to hundreds of students every year, passing classical liberalism off as the value-neutral "rules of the game." After my friend's comment, I began wondering what else Mankiw was saying—was he sending throngs of students into the world with the impression that the planet was "fine," while in other classrooms, we were slowly being crushed under the weight of the crisis' scale and gravity?

I showered, climbed into PJs, and made tea in my microwave, the rotating plate rattling in the otherwise silent room. As I stared at the mug, I felt that familiar sinking suspicion that Tom had been right about many things.

I was reminded of another class I'd been in, where the head of the Center for the Environment made the energy transition a question of numbers. For our final project, we were each given an Excel model built out with total carbon emissions per sector and various assumptions about what made them go up or down. Our task was to toggle—to play around with things like electric vehicle adoption rates, solar and wind energy installation, localization of supply chains—and chart a path to net zero carbon emissions by 2050.

The takeaway had been unavoidable: all of the paths were ridiculous. They required technology we didn't have, behavior changes that would be impossible to enforce in a democracy, and a whole lot of wishful thinking coded into columns and rows. What was trippy was thinking back on that class now that I knew the professor got research funding from oil and gas companies and opposed divestment. Did that make the spreadsheet's insights suspicious? I didn't think so. Because, as Tom had always argued, the evidence was clear: As much as we needed the government to stop helping Big Oil, we *did* need it to put money toward innovation. We needed the venture capitalists, the engineers, the Elon Musks; we needed everybody. Before, I'd conceded this begrudgingly; now, I felt it with a passion that was newly my own. We still didn't know how to replace cement with a building material that doesn't emit one ton of $CO_2$ for every ton of cement produced, how to make organic food on a massive scale, or how to make veganism affordable.

And yet it felt like so many of the adults who had the training to actually build a sustainable economy were also complicit in profiting off the old one. My professor seemed to regard the laws of the market like the laws of nature—austere, unchanging, beautiful. And, like Tom, he seemed convinced it was arrogant to think we could resist them.

It wasn't that I didn't "believe" in "capitalism," whatever that meant. It was just that I found it heartbreaking. It devalued everything I loved—trees, poems, women—and, in protest, I'd refused to learn any of its rules. Few of us activists had. Asset classes, exchange-traded funds, private equity, and capital markets were all stuffed away in a box that most of us resented—and for good reason—yet here we were, making specific demands of Harvard's investment professionals.

But the problem was bigger than that: the Green New Deal was painfully vague about how we'd reach the benchmarks it set, and I wondered if the people who wrote it knew how to force such drastic change upon a capitalist economy successfully. I, for one, certainly didn't; I knew far more about capitalism's abstract pitfalls than its concrete operations, and I had a feeling that the latter would be vital if we hoped to supersede one massive industry with another. I thought back to the night I'd sat sipping Tuskers with Tom and Ian as business terminology flew dizzyingly high above my head. How was I supposed to fend off Tom's consumer-centric arguments when I was in the midst of realizing and re-realizing just how naïve to the system I really was?

Suddenly, it made sense: of course, all the intellectuals, artists, and writers believed the world was going to shit—because it was leaving *us* and what *we* loved behind—while all the coders and entrepreneurs and venture capitalists fantasized about the possibilities in their Boulder incubators, all perked-out, optimistic, and thriving. I'd accused Tom of being siloed, biased by the mental models his entrepreneurship religion had imprinted. But was I just as guilty: implicitly inclined to accept that people more like me were the ones with the truest answers?

But at least Tom *cared*. At least he wasn't one of the thousands of students who walked past our posters and scrolled past our posts, vacillating in the vast and vague overlap between those who see the magnitude of the problem as overblown and those who've thrown their hands up in hopelessness—both of which seemed to give them license to ignore it. As wise as he was, Ralph Waldo Emerson didn't offer much practical guidance about how to pull off the whole energy transition thing. I would need to listen to people like Tom for that. And I had been, for months, because when they came from him rather than some old, well-adjusted white guy, I felt I had to confront them—to simmer in the scary possibility of their truth and recalibrate my worldview to make sense of them.

That night, I felt slightly betrayed by all those who chalked up any and all criticism of divestment to special interests and painting the entire adult world as a churning pit of moral depravity just as we were entering it. If we knew how to rout out systems of oppression on a ten-year timescale; if we knew of a viable and more just alternative for resource allocation than capitalism; if any semblance of sustainability could guide the gas industry through the process of abandoning its traditional business model and powering the world a different way—well, we'd be in a far better place. But as young people trying to suss out which adults (and institutions) are bullshitting and which ones might be onto something, we might do well to ask tougher questions.

For months, Tom and I been charging each other with dangerous and unforgivable breeds of myopia. But we'd both been naïve. We'd both been stubborn. And, in a way, we'd both been right.

# Tom

## Cambridge, United States
### APRIL

Have you failed? A friend asked me, a few days after my fight with Eve. We were discussing post-grad plans at the only teashop in Harvard Square that tourists hadn't yet discovered—Café Pamplona. I can't remember exactly why she asked me that question, only that it carried over into an image of Eve casting a shadow in the back of my mind.

We hadn't talked, we hadn't texted, we hadn't asked our mutual friends about each other. I could have, but I didn't ask Oliver if he'd talked to Eve when we met in the common room after cramming for finals. I didn't ask Mariko, Eve's roommate, when we met for our Sunday evening art board discussions at the *Harvard Advocate*.

*Had I failed with Eve?*

Maybe. I mean, what had I been trying to achieve? Had I been trying to make her see why she was wrong and I was right? Had I been trying to make her stop her climate activism? I couldn't place a finger on a single concrete thing. And what was I hoping to achieve from the op-ed? What was I trying to say: that activism was bad? No. After all, activism has done very many good things for the planet and has been a key pillar of the Pan-African movement, of which I've been a part throughout my life. What was it then?

Sure, I had grown frustrated with the tactics of climate activists—particularly in the US and UK—which had reduced the very complex goal of combating climate change to a false binary. But it was also personal. I was bitter, and Eve had become the embodiment of everything I disliked about the West and Western climate change activists, who, despite being so removed from the problem, so insulated from the real ramifications of climate change, demanded the most attention on the global stage.

But Eve did remind me of something I had been running away from—GreenChar had failed in its mission. And rather than deal with that, I had, over the years, built narratives around this failure, one being that activism was, in part, responsible. How else could I explain why, as of 2019, Kenya was still heavily reliant on fossil fuels, even after policy had been changed and clean cookstoves made affordable? I had felt firsthand what happens when the optimism of youth collides with the reality of the world, and I could see she was about to follow a similar path.

# Eve

## Cambridge, United States

### MAY

One morning in May, the campaign got an email. The school would be holding a public debate: the head of the Harvard Management Company—the group that invests the school's endowment—would be coming to campus, and we were invited, or challenged, to send someone to debate her.

We speculated. Perhaps the president had finally gotten tired of us. Or maybe this was his way of saying, "It's not me you should be after; it's her." We weren't sure, but Isa asked me if I'd do it. A bit taken aback, I said yes.

I decided that I'd open my speech with Tom in mind and acknowledge the most reasonable grounds for skepticism. Moving money out of traditional *exchange-traded funds* (ETFs)—bundles of stocks that give their owners a tiny stake in a broad swath of the economy—and into fossil-free ones had little impact when otherwise invested the same way, just minus certain industries. Additionally, it was tricky to tell what was truly "fossil-free"—and prison-free, and tobacco-free—in an investing landscape with tons of "green," "sustainable," and "ESG" funds that did nothing to actually expedite the energy transition.

The truth was that selling direct or indirect shares in fossil fuel companies often didn't do much of anything—and shareholder activism, which involved remaining a shareholder but advocating for change "from the inside"—could play an important, and sometimes even more impactful, role. In fact, some climate activists strongly felt it was a better strategy as they preferred to have someone in investor meetings hollering about climate change rather than nobody. As a large institutional investor, Harvard might just be heard. The rub was that given shareholders' ultimate interest in strong returns, it was hard to simply sit back and trust Harvard to act as an activist shareholder.

As it turned out, the Harvard Management Company's managing director, Kate Murtagh, was not the kind of character who made a particularly compelling villain. At least not for me. Somehow, despite years of conditioning around the facelessness of bureaucracy, I found myself beside a real, human woman who reminded me of my neighbor—the one I'd pass on the street walking her corgis. As I sat beside her, making small talk while waiting for the event to begin, I thought about Tom's favorite line, "Those closest to the problem are closest to the solution." I may have been pretty far from this problem's most vulnerable victims, but I'd always been quite close to those with the leverage to switch things up. That had always been the point.

I wore a blazer. It was my first time dusting it off since my high school Model United Nations club days, and it gave the day a fun but weirdly play-acting quality—as if I was back to representing Sierra Leone on questions of nuclear weapons and trying to win Best Delegate rather than attempting to inspire seismic shifts in the management of the world's largest university endowment. Compounding this feeling was the fact that my parents were in the audience. They arrived first (at least half an hour early) and settled into the back corner as we set up. My mom, who teaches sixth-grade history, must have dashed over just after school; I wondered if my dad, an entrepreneur, had moved around some meetings. They snuck little chances to meet my gaze, sending me grins and thumbs up. They were a pair of super-parents and always had been, rooting for me with glee but never pressure.

Ms. Murtagh, I imagined, wore a blazer every day. I pictured her at a standing desk on some 23rd floor, five days a week and sometimes Saturday—having woken up in a town like mine, driven a black Audi sedan to Starbucks, and confronted a seven-tabbed Excel spreadsheet with a venti latte in hand as the sun rose over the Financial District. Not today.

The event was being held in Emerson 101—the same one where we met for Politics of Nature. This fact—the Emerson bit, especially—struck me as almost too poetic to be real. The room became surprisingly full—this time, the audience had been promised a "debate" rather than a "panel."

The moderator began with a brief history of divestment, which was helpful. From the podium to my right, she talked about South Africa and tobacco and thus dispelled any notion that this was a rogue or novel idea. Ms. Murtagh was given the floor first. Despite the blood rushing to my head as I faced a packed room, I tried to listen, wondering if she would say anything that would force me to nix one of the points I had drafted. She didn't.

Then it was my turn. I began to read what I'd written. I'd been up half the night finishing it and had wished I could send it to Tom to get his thoughts. Digging through my memories of all our winding chats, I recalled the different genres of his doubts and tried my best to address them. I was so used to bracing for his replies that I felt almost discouraged when I finished speaking and found myself staring blankly at the clapping, smiling audience.

But just as I was getting ready to take a seat, a thin, balding man stood up from near the back of the room. He continued clapping. A few others joined him. I recognized his face; it was Jim Anderson—the legendary discoverer of climate change's destruction of the ozone layer—giving a standing ovation! And then came the wave of euphoria: the reminder that year after year, for a decade, this stubborn movement had been ebbing and flowing and never giving up.

Next, an organizer from the prison divestment campaign reminded us about the other morally bankrupt industry the school continued to invest in. Her name was Amber, and she was a law student. Her words left chills as another one of America's shortcomings settled over the crowd. The fact that prison companies are in the business of finding ways to increase the already outsized number of incarcerated Americans, that shareholders like Harvard were effectively cheering them on, was almost too absurd to believe, no matter how many times I'd heard it.

Next, philosophy professor Ned Hall wrapped things up with some old-school chalkboard action, walking us through the logical fallacies in each of the most common arguments against divestment.

Finally, questions. The hands shot up. I could almost feel the kinks forming between Ms. Murtagh's shoulder blades as fifty people vied to ask her why she woke up each morning and chose to destroy the planet and its Black and Brown communities. As the first question was asked, I wondered if she could hear it or if she was having one of those moments when everything sounds slow and underwater.

Though the question was unrelated, she opted to reiterate the "shareholder activism works" message. But at the next raised hand, she was pestered further by an audience member who had evidently not come to mess around; it was clear that while *I* would not be doing any "debating," the audience did not want to leave without some sparring. On question three, she dropped her ace. "I don't actually have the authority to sanction divestment," was the gist of it. "That's up to the Harvard Corporation, not the Harvard Management Company."

There was an uncomfortable murmur as everyone collectively wondered: So then, why are we all here, talking to you? You manage the investments but do not *manage* the investments, which means all of this has been more or less futile?

And just like that, it was over. We all shook hands, and then I headed back to hug my parents and friends. Tom's cynical voice—telling me this was just another extracurricular chance to dress up and exhibit poise and a command of the English language, to have loved ones stick around to hand you flowers when you emerge from backstage—lingered. But I felt lighter, calmer, as though some wild ride I'd been on had finally leveled

What We Can't Burn

off. My parents were beaming. One friend told me she'd shed a tear. It felt so good to hug them.

That evening, our camera guy, Campbell, who had helped me prep and been a comforting presence throughout the event, posted the video on YouTube. Without thinking, I sent a link to Tom.

# Tom

## Cambridge, United States

### MAY

I did not submit the op-ed for publication.

But I didn't tell Eve. We still weren't talking. Sometimes, I wondered if she woke up each day, scrolled through her newsfeed, checked her inbox, and then browsed *The Crimson*—waiting for it to pop up. Did her heart sink whenever she didn't see it? Had she written a counter article that was lying in wait, a rebuttal that would bring our months-long back-and-forth firmly into the public sphere?

But there was nothing. Nothing from me. Nothing from Eve.

Until one day, she sent me a link to a YouTube video on iMessage.

I didn't have to infer what it was about—it was in the link's description. It was a debate between Divest Harvard and its arch-nemesis, the Harvard Management Company. Each had selected—and I assumed battle-prepared—a representative. For Divest Harvard, that was Eve Driver.

I must admit, it was exciting to receive the link. One way or another, it seemed, Eve and I's back-and-forth *had* found a public sphere.

Rather than a feisty debate like those Eve and I had become accustomed to, I knew this would be a rather dull spectacle the moment the reserved moderator announced the rules of engagement: each party would get to speak uninterrupted.

Eve took the podium some twenty minutes into the ninety-minute video to a chorus of applause (her Divest Harvard comrades, I imagined). She was wearing a blazer; I hadn't seen her wear a blazer before. Her voice was firm but contrite. It lacked the fire and passion I had associated with her in the past months. It also didn't carry the shrill tone I imagined all activists had when they were "activisting." Where was the anger and the shouting? Where were the high-pitched rallying cries and impassioned rhymes? It was plain and simple rhetoric. I listened on.

Eve's points were expertly constructed, as if she were a lawyer making her opening arguments. She acknowledged what the opposition had said and then began rebutting these claims and making a clear case-by-case argument for divestment. I was surprised. I was impressed. And it hit me that some of what she said were lessons I had already learned the hard way at GreenChar—like the role of policy in cultivating an environment for socially-conscious enterprises to succeed. Though perhaps I hadn't fully appreciated them back then.

When we started GreenChar, we didn't have a clear path toward financial sustainability. Our main product was clean-burning charcoal. Our primary markets were low-income households. We could sell one kilogram for thirty cents, and our profit margin was only two cents. To reach sustainability, we had to sell at an extremely massive scale. One pro-bono sustainability consultant once described our challenge as having a bulky product with low margins. And those margins were taxed at 16 percent.

But we faced other challenges as well, like changing consumer behavior. How do you convince consumers to change their habits? Especially low-income consumers with fewer accessible options? Sure, they cared about the environment, but their bottom line was making ends meet.

The Kenya Climate Innovation Center, which had helped incubate Green-Char, came to mind. On the surface, the Center's mandate was to find, fund, and support clean energy ventures. They did this through financing, expert support, and connecting the different players in the market. However, they also pushed for policies that helped these ventures succeed, like abolishing the 16 percent Value-Added Tax (VAT) on clean energy products.

Policy and entrepreneurship were intertwined. They had been dancing together since my GreenChar days, and I had just not realized it.

———

There is a passage from *Pilgrim's Progress* where a man visits the House of the Interpreter as it's being swept. Dust fills the room, and everyone inside is choking until a woman sprinkles water on the floor, and the dust settles; all is well.

"Have you read *Pilgrim's Progress*?" I asked a friend at dinner that night. She said no, and I told her the story.

"Why are you telling me this?" she asked.

I chuckled. I realized that I had come to Harvard when the dust filled the room of my life. But the dust was slowly starting to settle.

Later that night, I "loved" the link Eve had sent on iMessage and texted her back, "You crushed it."

As I put my phone down, my mind was alive with thoughts and buzzing with images, both vivid and ephemeral. Everything felt magnified yet distant, like I was experiencing everything and nothing at all—caught in a stasis of emotion. I envisioned what had been, what was, and what might still be between Eve and me. In the weeks since our YardFest confrontation, my friendship with Eve seemed to wander a thin line between existence and non-existence. Friendships, especially those as deep as ours, assume new weights when tested. Conflicts become more than disagreements, and it feels as if the world shifts beneath you, pulling apart ties that once seemed unbreakable. Maybe what we believed we could not burn, we somehow did.

Yet, the heart of it remained. And I knew that it remained. Caught between everything we'd shared and the silence that followed was a friendship too complex to end but too wounded to simply mend.

# Eve

## Cambridge, United States

### MAY

The next morning, on my way to toast a bagel in the dining hall, I came across that day's *Crimson* lying on a table. I stopped to grab it when I realized Kate, Amber, Ned, and I were on the front cover! We were all lined up and looking very business-like. I sat down and skimmed the page.

The center story was standard coverage of the event. But on the right, in the Opinion section, there was a piece from the Editorial Board titled "In Support of Fossil Fuel Divestment." My body started to tingle. The piece began: "For a long time, we have staunchly opposed divestment as a practice. We've argued it just isn't practical: it won't really affect the market; it won't reverse climate change; it will hurt our endowment... But" it continued, "listening to our peers and reflecting on our values as a Board has led us to conclude that our past perspectives have become increasingly dated."

I read it over again as groggy students filed past. I pictured the other organizers spotting the paper in their various dining halls, stopping in their various Wednesday tracks, and feeling deeply proud of the way their hard work throughout Heat Week had paid off. Seven years after all of this began, the student consensus was finally catching up.

The feeling lasted only a moment before cynicism crept in. *Oh good,* I found myself thinking. *Now that we'd persuaded a group of students with no other goal than to estimate the right side of history and position themselves on it, what can't we do?*

Known for being generally liberal, the *Harvard Crimson* Editorial Board was kind of a low bar—so low I thought we had already cleared it. How many people even read *The Crimson* anyway? Still ahead of us was the problem of penetrating all the tall buildings in all the Financial Districts of all the cities full of people with silk sheets and comprehensive health insurance whose only prerogative was to be well-adjusted and efficient. And then, there was the glaring omission of private prison divestment. It felt almost worse than a rejection—like Amber's haunting words hadn't even warranted a reply. It made this little "win" feel exhausting—a reminder of how far we still had to go.

And just like that, my thoughts were back to Tom. As I considered the smallness of this moment, I realized I'd started to sound just like him. It was Tom, not me, who liked making snarky comments about *The Crimson's* narrow readership. Still, it made me chuckle; for all his undermining jokes, he seemed always to be quoting the paper's articles, betraying the fact that he was, in fact, an avid reader himself. I knew he'd spot the story. I knew he'd go, "Well, well, well," as he picked up the page, wry but pleased.

I realized then that in all our squabbling, I'd forgotten to thank him—for pushing me to find the guts to get into any of this stuff in the first place and for teaching me so much of what he'd learned about the world. There were still deep rifts between us and concerns on my part about the values he held and the ways he operated. The closer I got to him, the farther I got from a center within myself, and I was not yet sure how to protect myself from this feeling. But in that moment, I knew it was still worth trying. Despite it all, sitting there with my little copy of the paper, he was the first one I wanted to call. I was sure he would know exactly how I was feeling, and we'd laugh about the tough odds and then keep on going. Despite our differences, Tom seemed to understand me in a way no one else did, and that counted for something, if not everything.

Later that day, I called him and invited him to come to my family's home for dinner. I lived twelve miles away, not seven thousand: it was about time I returned the favor. He agreed.

As he pulled up to my house a few weeks later, I marveled that we had ever been able to meet—that we had both been born during a moment in history when humans had learned and not yet unlearned how to move across the planet, powered by a dangerous liquid that we had found under the ground.

# Epilogue

A year and a half after we graduated, Harvard announced it was divesting. Led by Kate Murtagh, the team at Harvard Management Company slowly began reducing the endowment's direct exposure to fossil fuels, and in September 2021, President Bacow pledged to let all remaining fossil fuel investments expire.

The campaign's most impactful period occurred during the months and years that followed the short stretch covered in this book. Led by students with support from faculty, alumni, and groups like Divest Ed and the Campus Climate Network, the campaign more than tripled in size and went on to pioneer new and bolder tactics. The disruption of the Harvard-Yale football game, for example, brought the movement to entirely new scales and stakes. It was followed by an innovative legal approach invoking the Uniform Prudent Management of Institutional Funds Act to argue that as a charitable institution incorporated in Massachusetts, it was unlawful for Harvard to invest in fossil fuels that cause climate risk. Ultimately, it was after years of cumulative pressure via increasingly creative channels that Harvard agreed to divest.

As campaign organizers always made clear, however, divestment itself was not the sole, or even primary, goal. Rather, its broader goal was to spark larger conversations and pave the way for real climate action and policy to become passable.

GreenChar's story was a helpful one to revisit after divestment was promised and the campaign began thinking more seriously about reinvestment. Once the Harvard Management Company committed to decarbonizing the endowment, the question quickly became: How does one build and scale a just and sustainable economy?

After Tom left for college, Ian redesigned their business model. What had failed the first time was not the process of turning the sugarcane waste into fuel but rather the idea that they could sell it to hundreds of thousands of households. The most glaring problem was the charcoal cartel. Backed by the terrorist group al-Shabaab, which in turn is backed by al-Qaeda, the cartel maintains a tight grip on the household fuel market not just in Kibera but throughout much of East Africa. If the fossil fuel industry in America plays dirty, this cartel plays even dirtier; after two of its men met with Tom in the opening pages of this book, Tom had real reason to believe his life was in danger if he chose to continue competing with them for a share of the household market.

Another fundamental problem was the partnership that committed GreenChar to selling clean cookstoves with their fuel. This kind of bundling is often smart, but the problem was pricing; for both GreenChar and its partner, Envirofit, to get their money's worth, they needed to sell the stoves for $30 each. But in the local market, no one wanted to buy a cookstove at that price. Even if the one they had was a bit smoky, it worked fine—and it's notoriously hard to convince consumers to change their behavior, especially when they're on tight budgets and the new product is both pricier and very different. In Kenya and everywhere, the energy transition is up against the truism that "old habits die hard."

However, with startups, failure is common, and adaptation is crucial. After GreenChar collapsed, Ian built a new company called Vuma Biofuels alongside a new co-founder, whom he met at Boulder's Watson Institute. It sold the same kind of sugarcane fuel but compressed it into the enormous bricks I saw at his factory. These bricks had to be big because instead of households, his new clients were institutions—factories and buildings with a large and consistent demand for fuel.

The good thing about establishing a model that is financially self-sustaining is that you can always go back and *add* the more mission-oriented dimensions. Once you've scaled up and brought your costs down, you are freer to make choices that align with your values. Vuma went on to primarily serve the tea, cement, pharmaceutical, and paper industries. In addition to creating lots of local jobs—providing an alternative to the monopolistic sugar industry—it also saved twenty-five trees worth of firewood for every ton of fuel it sold. Vuma estimates that it has saved about 150,000 trees so far.

The company ultimately reconnected with the consumer market as well, as lung diseases remain an urgent health problem. Its recent fundraising came from the Bestseller Foundation, Kenya Climate Ventures, and the Westerwelle Foundation. Vuma was acquired in June 2024 and Ian is working on a new biochar venture, one whose mission will focus on uplifting sugarcane farmers by sourcing waste directly from them.

A recurring and key tension GreenChar's and Vuma's work reveals is the one between "impact" investors and traditional, commercial investors. Put simply, the former prioritize impact—often because they're funded by independently wealthy individuals and can afford to operate without a laser focus on their bottom line. The latter work like standard businesses, which means they can only exist if they're making money. They might aspire to uphold certain environmental and social ideals or even change the world, but at the end of the day, they're not charities, and they need to get returns.

Universities are somewhere in the middle. They're closer to traditional investors in that they need to generate returns to fund research, pay their workers, recruit top academic talent, and offer financial aid. At the same time, they receive government subsidies for the social benefits their research and education offer. This fact became the basis for a creative legal strategy that the divestment campaign developed, claiming that Harvard's investments in fossil fuels were not just immoral but also illegal. They filed

What We Can't Burn

a complaint with the Massachusetts Attorney General, and Massachusetts State Representatives Michael L. Connolly and Erika Uyterhoeven introduced a bill that would have compelled the University to divest. Given the timing of these legal efforts and Harvard's divestment, many believe they played a pivotal role. (Other students interested in filing similar complaints should contact the Harvard divestment campaign and/or the Climate Defense Project.)

The flip side of that coin is that in some instances—such as Harvard's farmland investments—it's better to work with an investor with at least some mandate to be socially responsible than one with no mandate other than profit. When students visited and spoke with farmers in Brazil affected by Harvard's investments, they often heard the same message: we *want* investment, but we want *responsible* investment. As entrepreneurs who work their tails off to get funding know, "investment" does not always connote exploitation—capital is one of the most empowering yet unevenly distributed avenues to job creation and community development. The problems arise when those offering that capital are laser-focused on profit and unwilling to share the venture's rewards with those whose land and labor it depends on. For example, suppose Harvard (or the third parties managing its money) were to sell off all the farmland in its portfolio; that land might be bought by a private equity company that would adopt even more violent and extractive practices in the name of getting as much value from the land as possible. Sometimes, communities are better off putting pressure on an existing investor to improve its business practices—as these farmers were doing by reaching out to Harvard students—than demanding that the investor "divest." And while "respectful" business practices are always hard to define and vary depending on the constraints of the region and the industry, the same is always true: talk to the community; listen to them.

This is a steep uphill battle, but hope can be found in unexpected places.

Let's stick with the example of Brazil's commercial soy farms and the Indigenous land grabs and deforestation they are causing. With or without "responsible" investors in the mix, the fact is that global demand for soy (and therefore land for soy farming) is rapidly rising as populations grow bigger and richer in developing countries. Among other things, soy is a popular feed source for livestock, and as people get wealthier, they eat more meat, which means farmers raise more livestock and buy more soy.

Kenya is one of many places where this is happening. And as we know, meat is a central part of Kenyan culture, so the kinds of veganism and vegetarianism that are trendy in Western countries won't be widely adopted anytime soon.

On the one hand, this means that, unfortunately, global headwinds are moving against farmers like the ones who reached out to Divest Harvard. Even if Harvard were to do better—which it should—the bigger problem would remain.

At the same time, as Tom has always emphasized, hope can be found in creative entrepreneurship that cuts through these headwinds by taking a different tack. While working on this book and living in Kenya, we met a young entrepreneur named Talash Hujibers. She runs a small company directly competing with these big soy farms in Brazil. She produces an alternative livestock feed that is cheap, local, and sustainable. It requires very little land and water to make and also recycles food waste. Her secret? Maggots. She and her team farm flies, feed them decaying food, harvest their eggs, boil and dry them, and sell them to local pig, chicken, cattle, and fish farmers. She didn't set out to help out those communities in Brazil, but by rerouting the supply chain with a creative idea, she just might. The trick is scaling. Other insect protein companies, including Ynsect, AgriProtein, Entocycle, and Sanergy, are working on factory-farming these bugs using high-tech sensors and climate control to get the flies producing at maximum efficiency. If they succeed, the insect protein industry could help relieve some pressure on the soy industry.

But raising capital to build new things is hard—especially as a female entrepreneur and especially as a woman of color. Among the funding sources Hujibers has targeted is the Gates Foundation, which funds similar social ventures in Kenya and worldwide. In the US, Bill Gates is a voice in the climate conversation with plenty of detractors. Interestingly, in the introduction of his book *How to Avoid Climate Disaster*, he cites the fossil fuel divestment campaign for inspiring his work on climate. However, many changemakers and activists stress that a) billionaires should not exist, and b) they should not be trusted to use their wealth to "solve" climate change (or other justice issues) in responsible ways. While both Microsoft and the Gates Foundation deserve plenty of constructive criticism—particularly because Microsoft continues to donate to the political campaigns of Republican climate change deniers like Mitch McConnell and David Purdue—billionaire investors do play an important role in today's funding landscape. Remember the tension between "impact" investors and traditional, commercial investors? Often, the privately wealthy are able and willing to make investments with higher risk or longer timelines—but greater potential for impact—because they don't need to earn returns. One of the lead investors in Ynsect is the Creo Syndicate, a group of wealthy families that pooled their assets to focus on funding climate solutions—including ones that might not work. Likewise, Bill Gates' new Breakthrough Energy fund is putting billions of dollars toward developing technologies for things we still don't know how to do—such as making cement that doesn't emit a ton of carbon dioxide for every ton produced. Researching and developing these technologies may be too risky an investment for most traditional investors. It is essential that the US government raise taxes and fund this stuff, too, but in the meantime, it's exciting and long overdue to see billions of dollars pouring into climate innovation.

That being said, understanding the nuances of different investors' priorities is crucial for social entrepreneurs. Innovate Kenya, Echoing Green, and GreenChar's third investor, Africa Eats, offered money with slightly different strings attached. While one investor might be strict about measuring the social impact, another might focus more on profitability. While it may seem like the former priority is always better, sometimes it leads companies to design business models that will never be able to sustain themselves without a constant flow of grant money. This is tough because it means the founders will have to file frequent grant applications and rely on (often foreign) funders, and because it can sometimes screw up the local economy. For example, local fuel or stove companies with no foreign "impact" funding might get crowded out of the market by companies whose funding enables them to charge lower prices. Another pitfall is that measuring impact remains tricky. Not all investors vet their companies' claims about the scale of their impact, and when they do, they can get hung up on quantifying that impact in ways that may not reflect a complex reality.

On the other hand, when your investors only care about profits, it can be hard to stay focused on the mission you set out to achieve; you might have to make more decisions that prioritize your bottom line but sacrifice critical parts of your impact. When Eve first asked Tom about GreenChar, she'd been focused only on impact: on whether it was possible for a business to be "green" in a legitimate way. But if a company can't stay alive—if it's not "sustainable" in the profit sense of the word—then all of its potential impact is lost.

This is where governments can come in. Many world-changing innovations have emerged from science funded by the US Department of Energy. Tesla, for example, wouldn't be possible without government-funded research that would have been too risky to fund when considered solely from a business strategy perspective. After learning about this history, Eve went on to work as a policy advisor at the Department of Energy, helping develop the strategy for rolling out funding for new technologies in the Bipartisan Infrastructure Law. Governments can play numerous other roles as well, ranging from tax subsidies to carbon pricing, but only if the political will is there to support it—which brings us right back to the importance of grassroots organizing to sustain and grow the climate movement. Again and again, we can find the power that comes from interdisciplinary collaboration.

# Reinvestment Handbook

It can be hard to know where to start when thinking about divestment and reinvestment.

One of the cool things about the global fossil fuel divestment campaign is that it has served as a springboard for so many climate leaders. For example, after years of research, two former members of Yale's campaign, Gabe Rissman and Patrick Reed, co-founded **YourStake**, which sells a software that enables financial advisors to screen clients' portfolios according to very specific values. First, the clients fill out a questionnaire about what matters to them—what kind of a world they want their savings to be helping build or not build. Then, the software tailors their investments accordingly. It also spits out specific impact feedback—things like: X fewer asthma attacks, Y more meetings led by women, etc. The YourStake founders believe that it's one thing to tout your civic values on Instagram, and it's another to take a hard look at your own 401(k) or Roth IRA. Altogether, a whole generation that thinks this way has the potential to change the way that money moves and build deeper accountability for corporations. "Historically, social movements are powerful because they built political momentum that cashes out in the form of votes," Rissman says. "But what if the youth-led climate movement can also cash out in the realm of personal finance?"

**WeFunder** is another pioneer in this wave of converting people-power into financial capital. Ever heard of "equity crowdfunding?" It's when a startup raises money from lots of individuals rather than just one or two big firms. The idea is that sometimes there is an entrepreneur prepared to build something that she or he *knows* lots of consumers want, but can't find venture capitalists willing to get behind them. (The venture capital industry, which is focused on identifying new companies and giving them the money they need to grow, is predominantly white (78%) and male (89%). These investors are often accused of discriminating against founders who don't look and think like them.) WeFunder offers founders a platform for crowdfunding instead of (or in addition to) fundraising for venture capital. It's a powerful tool for democratizing the process of building a new economy.

But access to capital markets—the big money, coming from the big banks and funds—remains crucial for most companies to really scale. More and more financial institutions are trying to invest "sustainably," but the specter of "greenwashing" hovers over this conversation, as more and more funds are marketed as green while continuing to invest in fossil fuel companies. One group working to help us see through the BS is **FossilFree-Funds.org.** Run by the nonprofit **As You Sow**, they rate all funds based on a series of metrics to help the public tell: Has this money *really* been divested? Is this fund *really* devoted to building a sustainable economy? These questions are hard to answer, but this site is a good place to start.

It's also worth highlighting that in 2020, As You Sow also built out **PrisonFreeFunds.org** to answer the same set of questions for the prison and border industries. Check it out. But also keep in mind that obviously, at the risk of falling short in all the same ways the University did in its response to these dual campaigns, we have not done a good job of narrating, nor providing resources about, the prison divestment campaign. We also know that we are not the two narrators best equipped to tell the story of that campaign. Still, read on knowing that our focus has been narrower than perhaps it should.

As You Sow was also one of several signatories to an open letter circulated in 2018 pressuring the American company General Electric (GE) to pull out of a plan to fund Kenya's first coal plant. Together with other shareholders, As You Sow pushed GE to disclose why it was backing a project that, in addition to its negative climate impacts, clearly lacked local buy-in. Kenya's economy runs primarily on renewable energy already, so not only would the plant have set the country back in that regard, but this particular plant would also have polluted and destroyed a delicate ocean ecosystem. It was slated to be built near the island of Lamu, where it would have jeopardized the community's primary livelihood: fishing. However, the community organized and resisted. Forming a coalition called Save Lamu, the community enlisted the support of **Greenpeace Africa** and the Pan-African environmental legal team **Natural Justice.** They staged protests and fought the plant in court—and they won. Between this ruling and pressure on investors to pull out, the project was ultimately scrapped.

Still, Kenya's economy is growing quickly and new energy infrastructure is important. **Cross Boundary** is one energy investor leading the charge in a way we both admire. Focused on scaling renewables across Africa, they pay careful attention to risk, community buy-in, and effective public-private partnerships. **SunFunder** is another leader in financing solar energy in East Africa. Started through crowdfunding and focused on off-the-grid solar like the kind Tom's family relies on, it's focused on filling an important gap in financing: access to debt capital (funds raised through loans). Companies rely on both "equity" and "debt" capital to grow, and just reinvestment will require particular attention to the latter.

With all this in mind, we thought we'd throw out a few more specific ideas for anyone looking to build out a reinvestment proposal for their university (or any other portfolio). A key constraint to be aware of upfront: It's important to think about reinvestment across all of the "asset classes," which are specific categories of investments that are not interchangeable. Three that we'll look at are equities (stocks), fixed income (bonds), and real estate.

# Equities

Let's start with *exchange-traded funds* (ETFs). These are big bundles of stocks that span a wide range of industries. Because these bundles touch so many parts of the economy, they are low-risk; if one sector is struggling, another might be thriving, and they balance each other out. One of the challenges with divestment is that many fossil fuel investments happen not through direct investments in the companies themselves but through ETFs, which contain fossil fuel stocks along with many others. In recent years, however, new ETFs have been built that avoid fossil fuels and private prisons while still getting "broad exposure." **ETHO** from **Etho Capital** is one of them. It was founded by one of Tom's Echoing Green Fellowship peers, Ian Monroe, a professor at Stanford and supporter of divestment. ETHO can replace ETFs like the S&P 500 (though please do your own careful due diligence before making any personal investment decisions.)

We can also invest directly in sustainable companies once they "go public" and can be traded on the stock exchange. One company that inspires us (but is not yet public) is **BlocPower**. Founded by community organizer Donnel Baird, the company focuses on greening inner-city buildings in the US—while making them safer and creating jobs along the way. Baird is also on the Sunrise Movement's Board of Directors (see below). Public companies whose shares can be purchased as part of reinvestment strategies range from Tesla to Beyond Meat.

# Fixed Income

Then there's the "fixed income" asset class. In this one, investors expect small but reliable returns.

- Community Loan Funds. The **Ujima Fund** and **Calvert Impact Capital** operate two. These loan funds pool money from investors and offer small loans to communities typically excluded from accessing them. Small loans can change lives—they can help build small businesses, send children to college, and empower communities to transform themselves as they see fit. These loan funds are often backed by foundations (or the government), so the risk for investors is low. In other words, if folks default (fail to repay their loans), another institution will pay the investor back. Many financial advisors describe community loans as "low-hanging fruit" for reinvestment. It's an approach that was pioneered by the University of New Hampshire. For those universities that want to focus on local community empowerment, the **Opportunity Finance Network** offers a tool to help groups identify community loan funds (run by *Community Development Finance Institutions*, or CDFIs) This tool can be found at https://ofn.org/cdfi-locator.

- Blue Bonds. On the other hand, since we know the countries least responsible for climate change are bearing the brunt of its impacts, reinvestment campaigns may want to focus on moving resources into communities farther afield. **The Nature Conservancy** has pioneered one approach for doing so. Often, as was the case in Lamu, Kenya, local governments may *want* to preserve natural resources, but they may not have the funds to do so. The idea with some "blue bonds" is to do a "debt-for-nature" swap, whereby a foreign nonprofit or bank buys a country's debt and refinances it under the condition that they conserve a certain portion of their ecosystem. This bond was experimented with in the Seychelles, another island chain off East Africa, and it led to the successful conservation of an ocean ecosystem while relieving the country of some of its debt. Of course, there is plenty of room for this to go very wrong—at its worst, it can hitch poorer countries to wealthier ones in a kind of neocolonial power dynamic—but if it's entered into on terms designed for and by the indebted country, it can offer powerful results.

- Another bond idea is being developed by the team at **Blue Forest Conservation.** Under current capitalist rules, a forest has no value until it is cut down—which says a lot about why we're in this mess. This "Forest Resilience Bond" is trying to change that by bringing together stakeholders who benefit from healthy forests and getting them to collectively fund forest management upfront so that wildfires are prevented and everyone reaps the rewards.

- The trick with "green" and "blue" bonds is to make sure they are enabling conservation that would not happen otherwise. Not all do this. Often, companies or governments can separate out operations that can be defined as "green" in somehow—even though they are operations they would have done anyway—and then get financing for those operations with "green bonds." Even though money is being moved around, there is no real change in total carbon emissions.

———

Again, no matter how much divestment and reinvestment is done, it won't be possible to drive real change without building global political power that changes domestic and international policy.

Founded by Bill McKibben (founder of the divestment campaign), **350.org** has been a leader in this work. Its Kenyan chapter, **350 Kenya**, was instrumental in supporting grassroots resistance to the coal plant almost built in Lamu.

Likewise, in the US, the **Sunrise Movement** continues to be a powerful force for building and sustaining pressure for politicians to act on climate.

These ideas are non-exhaustive. One of the most beautiful aspects of the movement is its decentralization, so make sure to look for groups in your particular community. If one doesn't exist, consider starting one. This ecosystem is quietly growing every day.

# Further Reading

Here's a non-exhaustive list of the books that we mentioned and quoted throughout.

***Emergent Strategy*** by Adrienne Maree Brown
Brown is a thinker unlike any other we've read and brings together ideas about justice and the natural world in a fresh and unique way. This book discusses change of all kinds and how we can both cause and adapt to it. It draws upon science fiction and poetry to help us understand these wild times.

***Project Drawdown*** edited by Paul Hawken, lead writer Katherine Wilkinson
This book lists the most promising climate solutions we have today. "Agroforestry," a farming practice that Tom's dad happens to use, is one of the many techniques it references. It's important to remember that these types of solutions and practices aren't always deployed with the goal of curbing carbon emissions; for many farmers, they offer other benefits like improving soil health or generating more income.

***Sweetness and Power: The Place of Sugar in Modern History***
by Sidney Mintz
This book tells the story of sugar. There may be no other story that so clearly illustrates the relationship between colonialism, capitalism, food, and the environment. A possible exception may be Amitav Ghosh's *The Nutmeg's Curse: Parables for a Planet in Crisis.*

***Merchants of Doubt: How a Handful of Scientists Obscured the Truth on Issues from Tobacco Smoke to Global Warming*** by Erik
M. Conway and Naomi Oreskes
This book reveals the history of climate change denial in the US, chronicling a campaign that was carefully orchestrated and funded by the companies who wanted to keep selling oil.

***Changes in the Land: Indians, Colonists, and the Ecology of New England*** by William Cronon
This one digs into the history of settler colonialism in New England.

***Decolonize the Mind: The Politics of Language in African Literature*** by Ngũgĩ wa Thiong'o
This book informed how we wrote and structured the book you're holding now. It's about what anti-imperialism means today and the ways language has been a tool of colonization. We wrote this book in English, but this is Eve's first language and Tom's second—creating a fundamental imbalance in the authenticity with which we were able to express ourselves. We made this choice so as to reach the widest possible audience, but this comes with notable pitfalls.

***Unbowed: A Memoir*** by Wangari Maathai
Wangari Maathai was a Nobel-prize-winning Kenyan environmentalist. As the first woman from East or Central Africa to earn a PhD and the first female professor in Kenya, her memoir is both a story of courage and a

book full of wisdom about taking on environmental challenges. Maathai's priority was always planting trees.

### *Windfall: The Booming Business of Global Warming* by McKenzie Funk

We didn't reference this book, but it did crystallize some of the stakes of our conversations. Among many other things, *Windfall* tells the story of Shell Oil's futurists, who, in 2008, looked ahead and envisioned the future of the oil industry in light of global warming. They devised and publicly released two potential scenarios—named, cryptically, Blueprint and Scramble—which told different stories of the world up through 2050. In the Blueprint scenario, world leaders acted quickly: an international system of carbon pricing created strong incentives that accelerated the development of clean energy, carbon capture technology improved so that fossil fuels could be burned more cleanly, and warming was capped at 1.5 degrees despite rapidly growing energy demand in countries like China and India. Meanwhile, Scramble, which is now understood as the scenario more closely resembling today's reality, was far more grim. Among various obstacles to the carbon pricing and regulations detailed in Blueprint, one challenge jumped out to us. Quoting the Scramble report, Funk writes: "In Scramble, climate campaigners get louder, but 'alarm fatigue' afflicts the general public. International discussion on climate change becomes bogged down in an ideological 'dialogue of the deaf' between the conflict-ing positions of rich, industrialized countries versus poorer, developing nations—a paralysis that allows emissions of atmospheric $CO_2$ to grow relentlessly." Reading this, we felt like Shell and its futurists had seen our tiffs coming. Not really ours, of course, but the ones that mattered—the ones that have made so many international climate conferences fall flat. They even foresaw and perfectly described the "dialogue of the deaf" that we became caught in—in which we found ourselves able to hear but never really listen.

***Braiding Sweetgrass*** by Robin Wall Kimmerer

This book is a gorgeous tribute to the land to which Kimmerer is indigenous and a powerful call to rekindle our relationships with whatever land we now inhabit. Gratitude, more than anything else, will help us avert ecological catastrophe. Kimmerer suggests gratitude, community, and hope.

***How to Avoid a Climate Disaster*** by Bill Gates

Gates offers what some would call a "techno-utopian" view of climate solutions, but we feel that his push to invest in innovation is crucial. Cement is a powerful example; in many parts of the world, it is the best building material we have, and yet, by the laws of chemistry, there is a 1:1 cement-to-carbon dioxide ratio. We need to develop a replacement if we're going to get ourselves out of this. Gates offers a survey of progress toward net-zero emissions across various sectors and then explores whether lagging technology or "green premiums"—making the green options prohibitively expensive—are the biggest barriers in each case.

***Dirt Road Revival: How to Rebuild Rural Politics and Why Our Future Depends on It*** by Chloe Maxmin and Canyon Woodward

The two founders of Harvard's fossil fuel divestment campaign have gone on to do big things; with Woodward as her campaign manager, Maxmin won a seat in the Maine State Senate, flipping a red district and learning a lot about building long-lasting progressive movements that genuinely resonate with rural communities. Much like we did, these two found the divestment campaign to be a powerful yet limited way to mobilize people around the climate crisis. This book is an inspiring yet practical guide for applying community organizing to political campaigns in ways that translate into legislation.

———

More work is published every day, giving us more words of warning as we navigate this moment. However, we must be careful as we read; it's important that we conserve our energy, direct our hope, and see through empty promises. Still, we are lucky. As more stories surface, testifying to the hard work happening on both local and global levels, we become witnesses to new ways of living together on our beautiful but fragile planet. These stories sustain us and keep us feeling inspired. We hope they get told and heard just as often as the tragic ones.

# Acknowledgments

This book wouldn't exist without Eve. Her vision for how our friendship—and sometimes lack thereof—could serve as a template for many. Her patience with me, even when I "abandoned the English language" in a fit of Pan-Africanism and Ngũgĩ Wa Thiong'o love. Her resolve to get going—in the face of many rejections—until we got this book published. Thank you for the gift of writing this together and sharing so much of our lives in this process.

A heartfelt thanks to our early readers: Oliver, Jana, and Julia. Your encouragement kept us writing.

To Kendi, who ensured I never got distracted; Soni and Netsanet, who gave this book legs in Kenya; and all the Shamirians who supported this project and inspired us to envision the world as it should be, not as it is—thank you.

Jess and Ed, no one weaves together a story like the two of you, thank you for shaping this book.

—Tom

First, a round of applause to those who led Harvard's fossil fuel divestment campaign to victory. Some of the many, many individuals to celebrate include: Ilana Cohen, Claire Pryor, Caleb Schwartz, Nuri Bhuiyan, Isa Flores-Jones, Georgia Bowder-Newton, Kari Traylor, Isaac Ortega, Julia Hynek, JD Deal, Eva Rosenfeld, Sofia Shapiro, Phoebe Barr, Mei Collins, Carl Denton, Caleb Schwartz, Chloe Maxmin, Canyon Woodward, Aryt Alasti, Jim Engell, Virginie Green, Jim Anderson, Ned Hall, Joyce Chaplin, James Recht, Richard Thomas, Nicholas Watson, Jane Mansbridge, Stephen Marglin, Shoshana Zuboff, Eric Chivian, Caren Solomon, Timothy Wirth, Todd Gitlin, Stephen Heintz, Joan Hutchins, Bevis Longstreth, Gina McCarthy, Bill McKibben, Kat Taylor, Tom Oliphant, Darren Aronofsky, John Harte, and countless others whose paths did not cross with my own.

Next, applause for our publishers, Jessica and Ed. Thank you for showing us what it looks like to be entrepreneurs, activists, and academics all at once. You brought profound empathy and vision to this book, which both tightened and expanded it in ways we never could have imagined. Thank you for believing in us and making our dream a reality. I will forever consider it a privilege to have been part of Westwood's journey from the near-beginning. I believe so deeply both in your mission and in your unique ability to make it happen.

Thank you also to Westwood Press and the team that brought this book together: cover designer Jack Smyth, copyeditor Chelsea Jackson, and interior designer Morgane Leoni. Thank you for capturing the spirit of the book in your art and pulling it together so beautifully. And thank you to our agent, Andrea Blatt, for being one of this book's first and most empowering champions, and for being the wind in our sails during challenging phases.

Next, a special thanks to those who read the book, proposal, or query letter at early stages and offered their feedback or support—including Lisa Driver, Tim Driver, Caio Driver, Emily Moore, Anne Midgette, Claire Bidwell-Smith, Abigail Simon, Emily Corrigan, Val Elefante, Oliver Piltch, Emily Koch, Aja Two Crows, Jules Kardish, Julia Bunte-Mein, Gracie Brett,

Ryan Jones, Josh Karp, Matt Miller, Michael Ellsberg, David McCullough Jr., Stephen Shafer, Chip Fisher, Devi Lockwood, and Meghan Maguire. When this book was just the tuft of a dream, your support meant so much.

Next, gratitude for the many places from which this book was born: Cambridge, Ipswich, South Dartmouth, Naushon, Wellesley, Beacon Hill, Nairobi, Shompole, and Brooklyn. Also, the places where we spent time in the book itself: Franconia, Cambridge, Kisumu, and Awendo. In addition to my gratitude for these places and their distinct energies and ecologies, I'd like to acknowledge the ancient stewardship of these places by Indigenous peoples including: the Massachusett, Wampanoag, Pawtucket, Wabanaki, Lenape, Luo, Maasai, Kamba, and Kikuyu.

Finally, there is a quote I like from a climate writer named Mary Anaise Heglar. It is about the world she wants to build out of the chaos of this one. Sure, she thinks it's worth doing what we can to stop climate change in its tracks. But more than that, she says, she dreams of "a world where we might still have the storms, but we know better how to take care of one another." In that spirit, my deepest gratitude is to my parents, family, roommates, friends, coworkers, and loved ones who cared for me and let me care for them all this time. I will refrain from listing you all by name, but I trust that you know who you are. Far beyond anything written in this book, you have shown me what kinship and community can be when we earn each other's deepest trust—when we let each other grow and evolve across time, give ourselves and each other the benefit of the doubt, and challenge each other from a shared foundation of integrity. Since graduating, I have been blessed to live, work, and grow with people who have taught me new modes and standards of care, and shown me that especially in a warming world, we must learn to weave ever-tighter fabrics of community around us.

My last note is to Tom. After the period we narrated, the story of our friendship got more complicated, more challenging, and in many moments, more beautiful. No matter how our story unfolds from here, I will forever cherish the memory of the night I turned 26 with you. Every day, bridges burn down between people who care for each other. But as we walked along the Hudson River in the near-dark, in tears of laughter about your overuse of the word "motif," I almost couldn't hold in me all of the aching gratitude that for all those years, we had held ours together.

—Eve